1

Into the Mystic
by
Keith Green

This book is dedicated to my mother, Eileen whose Loyalty and dedication to her country helped to defeat the enemy for peace and freedom from oppression.

And to the countless women of the Secret Service during the Second World War. Without recognition, they listened in silence, coded in secrecy, and enabled us to gain the upper hand and win the war.

May their stories no longer remain hidden in the shadows.

Tom and Eileen Green's Wedding picture in front of the Wandsworth Town hall on Jan 13, 1940.

Cast of Fictional Characters

Albert Schulte

John Mitchell MI5

Lieutenant
Arthur Coleman

Angus Hines

Finlay

Professor Beattie

Hamish McTague

Bruce

Professor Richardson

Major Williams

Jan van Rijckenborgh

Miss Leitch

1

The Conductor's Secret

The rain came down in sheets, drumming against the roof of the double-decker bus lumbering through bomb-scarred London streets. Eileen tugged her conductor's cap tighter over her dark hair and moved down the aisle, balancing as the bus rocked over the rough pavement, collecting fares, issuing tickets and clipping ticket stubs. It was March 1941, the end of one of the worst winters on record, a winter that seemed to go on forever. The passengers hunched in their seats, coats pulled tight against the chill, eyes set on some distant point beyond war-torn buildings and barrage balloons tethered like swollen spectators in the sky.

"Oxford Circus!" she called crisply above the din, her voice calm above the roar of the engines. Even amid destruction, her steady presence cut through the thick diesel fumes, offering a sense of safety and familiarity.

She paused by an older man in a worn tweed jacket who fumbled for change with gnarled fingers. "Keep your shilling today, Mr. Porter," she said with a slight nod. "Wet enough without adding an open window to it." His surprised chuckle was lost to the roar of an airplane overhead, a reminder of how close the war loomed.

Among the many faces that came and went each week, one appeared with peculiar regularity a man in a dark overcoat who always carried the *Daily Telegraph* to read on his journey. He rode the bus often but never seemed to have the same destination. He made Eileen a little nervous; then one day he boarded the bus, but this time sat down near the rear, where Eileen sat between stops.

"Good morning. My name is Albert," he said.

"Good morning, I'm Eileen," she replied suspiciously.

"You don't look well," he said. Eileen explained to him that she'd had no choice of jobs and had to endure feeling sick all day from the diesel fumes and the motion of the bus.

"You dropped your paper yesterday," she remarked.

"I wondered what happened to it," he said, "Do you like crosswords and puzzles?"

"Yes, why do you ask?"

"The crossword book in your pocket."

"Oh, yes, it takes my mind off the war, and I love to work on the *Daily Telegraph* cryptic crossword puzzles; crossword books are so hard to come by these days."

Suddenly, he rose. "This is my stop." He stepped off in a hurry and disappeared into the crowded streets. The newspaper, folded open at the crosswords, slipped from his coat pocket, tumbling to the floor, its pages flapping like startled pigeons.

Eileen retrieved it to return it. As she smoothed the wrinkled paper, her eyes caught a note in the margin - a series of numbers inked in neat script alongside a notice for bomb shelters. The incident stayed with her long after she handed control of Route 72 over to the next shift.

She walked home briskly through the late afternoon gloom, her thoughts snagging on that cryptic note.

Numbers fascinated her; they were constants in a world of chaos and uncertainty. She could recall each digit the man had written without effort, and as she made her way home, they tapped a rhythm in her mind.

She lived with her parents and infant son in a modest flat on the ground floor of a building that had seen better days. The windows were crisscrossed with tape, protection against the bomb blasts that had already scarred parts of South London. Inside, the rooms were tidy but sparsely furnished, reflecting Eileen's parents' practical nature more than any sense of impermanence or comfort.

As she entered the flat, her father, Claude, was reading the *Daily Telegraph*, and her mother, Jessie, was preparing the afternoon tea. "It's awful weather out there, my dear. You should get into something more comfortable before you join us for tea. Jeffery's fine. I just put him down. If you wait a few minutes, you can kiss him without waking him."

In the bathroom, Eileen peeled off her damp uniform and slipped into her housecoat and slippers. Then she stood a few moments in the dark bedroom listening to her three-month-old breathe.

During tea, they discussed what had been available in the shops and what streets had been damaged the night before. Eileen said, as she often did over her tea, that she missed her husband, Tom. He'd volunteered for the Royal Army Service Corps as a driver, and not long after their baby was born on December 7, 1940, he had been sent to Egypt.

Claude and Jessie retired to their bedroom early, leaving Eileen to give Jeffrey his last feeding. Finally, when he was settled, Eileen had a chance to examine the numbers on the newspaper closely. She reached for a pencil and paper, jotting down the sequence of numbers: 34 18 62 45. She was curious, more curious than usual. It wasn't just the numbers themselves, it was the odd way they had been left for her to find. She tapped the pencil against her chin, considering their significance. Perhaps a cipher of some kind, like the codes she'd read about in the newspapers. Was it an accident, or was she supposed to do something with it?

She had wanted to change jobs ever since she started on the buses. As she had explained to Albert, the heavy fumes of diesel in the air, mixed with the sharp, metallic scent of bus exhaust, made her stomach churn. But in wartime, women needed to keep things going on the home front, and they had little choice of jobs. Quitting a job could lead to a jail sentence because the government had strict measures to maintain enough workers for the war effort. Munitions factories, transport, and farms needed people as much as the armed forces did. Quitting a job was seen as hindering the war effort.

Several days passed. Most days, Albert rode her bus. Then one Friday evening, "Euston Station," he said. This time, his departure was interrupted. A motorcar stalled directly in front of the bus, drawing a chorus of horns and angry shouts. Instead of slipping away, he turned abruptly and handed Eileen an envelope, his fingers gloved and deliberate.

"For your trouble, Eileen." His voice carried a hint of something, a challenge, perhaps. Then he disappeared into the confusion outside. Inside the envelope was a single slip of paper. Typed across it: **HM Treasury**.

A chill that had nothing to do with the weather ran through her as she reread the message. Eileen's heart skipped a beat or two as she folded the note carefully and placed it in her pocket. She gripped the polished rail of the bus for support, feeling the hum of its engine beneath her feet as it lurched back into motion. The city blurred past in streaks.

That night, she made the decision to quit her job on the buses. The next day, she arrived early at the bus terminal, before the 7:00 a.m. starting time. Holding herself straight so that no one would notice her nervousness, she approached her boss. "I'm sorry, but I can't stand the fumes any longer. I have to quit."

14

"You can't quit, Mrs. Green. I'll have to report you. You'll go to jail."

"Fine," she said. "At least I won't feel sick all day." Placing her badge and cap on his desk, she left.

The next morning, as she was sitting in the kitchen with her tea and toast, there was a knock at the door of the flat. She opened it to find a man in uniform, his expression stern.

"Who is it, dear?" her mother asked from the sitting room.

"Eileen Green?" the man asked, though it was hardly a question.

"Yes," she replied, steeling herself.

"I'm to escort you to your interview," he said briskly, showing her an official letter from the Admiralty. "No time to waste."

She hesitated briefly, then nodded, grabbed her coat, and kissed her mum and dad, saying, "I'll explain at teatime."

With that, she left. The ride in the government-issued car was silent. The city seemed almost peaceful in the early morning light. She clutched the note in her pocket as if it were a lifeline.

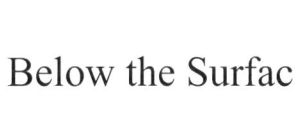

2

Below the Surface

They arrived at Whitehall, the home of the Treasury Department. There were security guards at the entrance, and Eileen worried. How much trouble was she in for quitting the bus conductor's job? She was escorted down a long hallway, with the clatter of typewriters filling the air, mingling with the low murmur of tense conversations.

The man led Eileen to a small office with frosted glass walls. Inside, a woman in a crisp military uniform sat behind a desk, flipping through a file. She looked up as they entered, her sharp gaze appraising Eileen before she spoke.

"Mrs. Green, I'm Major Lambert," she said without preamble. Her voice was clipped, efficient. "Please sit."

Eileen took the chair opposite, her face calm, she hoped, despite the anxious flutter in her stomach.

"I understand you've had a change of employment status?" Major Lambert continued.

Eileen nodded. "It seems I have."

"Good," said Lambert, allowing herself the slightest smile. "We don't have time for second thoughts here. You've been selected for an assignment with one of our most confidential divisions. You've been brought here because we believe you have certain skills, skills that are desperately needed if we're to win this war."

Eileen considered the words carefully. "You mean… numbers?"

The Major's expression remained enigmatic. "And your conduct under pressure. But yes, we have noticed your affinity for numbers."

She pushed the file across the desk. "The work is sensitive. It will require absolute discretion and commitment. You may not discuss your work with anyone. This is not a decision to make lightly."

Eileen glanced at the open folder. Her own name was there, typed neatly among other details of her life. She felt exposed, as if they had decoded her before she'd even begun.

"I'm ready," Eileen said, her voice steadier than she felt. "What do you need me to do?"

Major Lambert closed the file with a nod of satisfaction. "For now, follow Mitchell. He will take you where you need to go."

They emerged into a nondescript hallway on the ground level. Eileen was then led to an underground operations centre, where she was inducted into the Secret Service. Mitchell stayed close at her side, guiding her through each step with quiet efficiency. The signing of papers felt monumental, each stroke of the pen binding her to this clandestine life. Eileen pressed her fingers to an ink pad and then to a card, and the black smudges were a stark reminder of the indelible commitment she was making. When she received her badge, a small metal rectangle stamped with an identification number, it felt heavier than she expected.

Mitchell said, "Follow me." He led the way down a corridor and stopped in front of a heavy door, ushering Eileen inside. She blinked, adjusting to the dim light of a vast, vaulted room.

Unlike the bustling activity outside Major Lambert's Office, this space held the stillness of concentration. Rows of long tables lined the room, each piled with documents and cryptic charts.

"This is where you'll begin," Mitchell said, his voice echoing slightly. "The Naval Stores Office."

Eileen hesitated, taking in her surroundings. The people at the tables were mostly women, their faces drawn as they worked through the mounds of information before them. The scratch of pencils and the occasional rustle of paper was broken only by her whispering voice.

"Naval Stores?" she asked, feeling an unexpected thrill.

"Coordinating supply chains for the Merchant Navy," Mitchell replied. "Everything you do here will be highly classified."

He led her towards a cluster of desks in one corner. "This is your station. You'll be assigned tasks shortly." He paused, his eyes meeting hers, underscored the importance of her new role.

"Remember, Mrs. Green, secrecy is paramount."

Eileen nodded, the seriousness of what lay before her settling in. She watched as Mitchell turned and left, disappearing into the shadows of the hallway.

She sat at her desk, absorbing the tense atmosphere around her. Here it was, an opportunity to contribute directly to the war effort in ways she never imagined. Her fingers itched to begin, to immerse herself in the coded universe spread out before her.

A woman with severe bangs and a no-nonsense demeanour approached, dropping a stack of papers on Eileen's desk without breaking stride. "Shipments out of Liverpool," she said curtly. "Need them organized by noon."

Eileen picked up the first sheet, her mind already whirring with patterns and possibilities. She worked methodically through the morning, losing herself in the intricate dance of logistics and numbers. Each shipment coordinated, each code deciphered was a blow struck in the hidden war she now fought. Hours slipped by unnoticed until a distant rumble jolted Eileen back to her surroundings. The others barely glanced up, accustomed to the sound of explosions echoing from the city above. She forced her attention back to her work, but her thoughts lingered on what this new life would demand of her.

As the day wore on, Eileen's meticulous nature served her well; she identified gaps and inconsistencies with an ease that surprised even her. When Mitchell reappeared at dusk, she had completed more than she thought possible for her first day.

He surveyed the papers spread across her station with a nod of approval. "You've done well," he said, his tone less formal than before.

"Thank you," Eileen replied. One of the other women paused near Eileen's desk, her expression curious and kind.

"First day?" she asked, offering Eileen a biscuit wrapped in paper.

Eileen accepted it gratefully. "Yes," she admitted. "It's... quite something."

The woman nodded with a knowing smile. "I'm Peggy. Been here three months and still pinching myself." She gestured to the documents scattered across their desks. "Just think what it all means for our boys out there."

Eileen warmed at Peggy's words, a connection to the larger mission. She was about to respond when Mitchell's voice interrupted.

"Mrs. Green, it's time we took you home."

Eileen gathered her things, only now realizing how tired she was.

March winds and rain were still pounding London, and it was bitterly cold. The trip back was as silent as the morning's had been, but her mind was far from still. She replayed the day's events, imagining that her work was helping her husband, Tom. As they neared her flat, London's night air was heavy with the scent of smoke and anticipation.

As the car pulled away, Eileen looked down; tucked into the edge of the door was an envelope. As she opened the flap, she read: "You left this on the bus. Burn after reading." Eileen tucked the envelope into her coat and turned to see the official car disappearing into the fog like a ghost.

Entering the warm comfort of their flat, Eileen found her mother, Jessie, busy getting tea while also juggling her three-month-old grandson, Jeffrey.

Her father looked up from his paper and said, "Would you care to elaborate on this morning's sudden departure?"

"I'm sorry. I meant to tell you that I quit the bus conductor job, and they told me that I would have to go to jail; so I didn't want to alarm you." Eileen took the baby from her mother's arms and rubbed her cheek against his soft skin. She warmed a bottle and fed Jeffrey as Jessie put plates on the table.

"So, was that a constable at the door this morning?" he said anxiously.

"No, it was the military police escorting me to Whitehall."

"Whitehall? Isn't that the Treasury Department?"

"Yes, because of my clerical experience, they have me working as a clerk in the Naval Stores Office."

"Well, that's a relief," said Jessie. Jessie placed a tea plate in front of her. "Eat before you fall asleep where you sit."

Eileen laughed softly and obediently picked up her scone. Everything was rationed, so the tea bags were often left over from the morning, but she hardly noticed. She ate with an appetite she didn't realize she had, consuming the biscuits and dabbing a little marmalade on the scone.

"You're to be careful, Eileen," said Claude, raising his head from the newspaper he had spread on the table.

"I'll be careful," she assured him. "It's mostly paperwork. I'm quite safe."

Claude didn't look completely convinced but nodded.

Home was a balm after the day's concentration, yet Eileen felt the restless pull of her new duties even now.

Jessie watched her with a warm smile on her lips. "You look different already," she teased. "Perhaps a new hat is in order for this new life of yours?"

Eileen grinned, feeling for the first time in months that everything around her, Tom, family, duty - was connected in some meaningful way. Tom's departure had left a void, a silent ache in her daily life. Eileen missed his familiar presence. His letters arrived infrequently, filled with brief, loving messages and occasional blacked-out sentences. He couldn't tell her where he was or what he was doing. She cherished each one. The weight of his absence drove her. She wanted to excel in her new job.

As they finished eating, the conversation shifted to the day's events: shortages in the shops, news from the front. Claude had worked on the White Star Line as a pastry and dessert chef. His voyages had been long and arduous, with long days at sea. He had sent postcards when possible. But all of that was gone with the war, so he'd found a job as a milkman. Eileen joined in, telling about the traffic jam on Horseferry Road that morning, but she sensed her parents' unspoken worry hovering in the air like the cigarette smoke.

Later, as she tucked the baby into his basket for the night, Eileen slipped the envelope from her coat and retreated to their room. She waited until she heard her parents' murmurs fade into the stillness of sleep. Then, with unsteady hands, she opened the envelope. The contents were as precise and cryptic as the work she'd done that day: addresses, times, coded references to ships and cargo. They demanded immediate attention. Eileen smoothed the paper and committed each detail to memory before feeding it to the hungry flicker of a candle flame. She watched the edges curl and blacken, thoughts drifting to her husband Tom in some distant port. The war had scattered them into separate worlds; yet she felt their paths converging here in these secret tasks. Her station at Naval Stores was a lifeline tethering him to her.

Sleep came fitfully, images of maps and ship manifests weaving through her dreams. She woke with a start when the air raid siren split the night air. Claude appeared in the doorway.

"Hurry, get under the bed with the baby. There's no time to reach the shelter."

Huddled together, they prepared themselves for the noise and fear. The house was near Clapham Junction and the main rail lines, which were frequent targets for German bombings. Suddenly, there was a terrific crash, and Eileen couldn't move. She could hear her mother sobbing and her father's murmurs, but she couldn't move. The bed was crushing down on her. Jeffrey was frighteningly still. She had no idea how long she lay there, calling out when she thought she heard voices. The man who finally lifted the bed said they'd been there for eight hours.

"You're lucky to be alive, and in this cold," one of the rescue workers said. "By rights, you all should have been killed."

The bomb had demolished the back of the house, burying them under rubble. The house was destroyed, and her son was dead. Eileen didn't feel lucky at all. She felt nothing, just cold and numb.

Tom came home for a week on compassionate leave; then it was back to the war for him. They never talked about Jeffrey or that night again.

Now, Eileen was more determined than ever to do her part in the fight against Hitler. She returned to work the following week. Her parents were worried about her working in the Naval Stores Department. They did not know how protected the area where she worked was, and she couldn't tell them.

Instead, she said, "I need to be there, to feel like I'm doing something meaningful, that I'm still a part of this life."

Jessie and Claude moved north to Preston, in Lancashire, and stayed with friends; Eileen moved in with her older brother, Leslie, and his wife, Frances, who had a two-bedroom flat that had so far survived the Blitz. Leslie's shoe repair shop had been bombed out. He had been too young to fight in World War I and was now too old for World War II, so he had joined the fire department. Eileen was grateful for her brother's help, but had more pride than gratitude and found herself irritated by the arrangement. She was glad to get back to work.

As the days and weeks wore on, the memory became an old wound, but it hadn't lost its sting. Eileen often lay sleepless under the safety of blackout curtains, the sights and sounds of that brutal night returning each time she closed her eyes.

Each dreary London dawn ushered in a monotonous ritual. The city felt ghostly, half-real beneath its shroud of mist and smoke. Each day, Eileen walked quickly to catch her bus to Whitehall, pulled by a sense of urgency. Peggy and the other women in the war room hunched over their desks in concentration. Each morning, the same woman handed her another stack of documents as soon as she sat down. From time to time, Mitchell passed by, his nod efficient and approving. The routine felt almost familiar now, a rhythm she could lose herself in.

The hours and days vanished into the chaos of their work, the outside world reduced to muffled echoes of war. Eileen thrived on the pressure, her instinct for patterns and precision sharper than ever. One day, as exhaustion crept in, Peggy appeared at her side with a cup of tea.

"You're a natural," Peggy said, her eyes warm and teasing.

Eileen smiled, accepting the tea gratefully. "I just hope I can keep up," she replied.

Peggy laughed. "You will. We all manage somehow."

Eileen returned to her work, buoyed by Peggy's confidence and the sense of purpose that filled their workspace.

Her thoughts drifted to Tom often, wondering if he felt the strain of war as keenly as she did. Mitchell approached again late in the afternoon, and Eileen had to blink herself back into the present. His expression was as inscrutable as ever, but she thought she detected a hint of approval.

"Very good, Mrs. Green," he said. "I'll see you home."

The trip was swift, and the familiar streets blurred past. Eileen was in a haze of fatigue and determination. Mitchell kept his eyes on the road, leaving Eileen alone with her thoughts. Once again, in the corner of the doorway was an envelope. This one thicker.

As soon as the car was gone, she hurriedly stooped, slid the envelope into her pocket and took a deep breath. Inside, Francis was knitting by the wireless and Leslie was reading the paper.

"Working you hard?" Leslie remarked as Eileen came into the room.

"You know how it is," she said lightly, shifting her coat to conceal the envelope within its folds.

"Always something more to do."

The next day, she went to her underground world, thick with the hum of machinery and voices that echoed off the concrete walls.

"Eileen," Mitchell met her at the door. "Follow me, I have a new assignment for you." He led her to a stark room lined with filing cabinets and with maps pinned to every surface. A heavy wooden table dominated the centre, laden with stacks of papers and telephones. The atmosphere crackled, an invisible current that set Eileen's heart pounding.

"Welcome to your new post," Mitchell said. He gestured for her to take a seat at the table. Eileen sat down, taking in her surroundings with a mixture of awe and apprehension. She was at the nerve centre of something vast and intricate, a web she had only glimpsed until now.

25

An older man in a crisp suit entered, his expression severe beneath rimless glasses. He wasted no time on introductions. "You're here because we expect the highest level of commitment," he said, his voice crisp. "This is the Map Room, and everything that passes through must be handled with absolute discretion." Eileen nodded, absorbing the gravity of his words. Mitchell's approving nod was all the acknowledgement she needed to know there would be no turning back now.

"Major Lambert will brief you further," Mitchell said, dismissing her with a nod.

Eileen rose, clutching her documents and headed down the corridors to Major Lambert's office.

"Mrs. Green, you've joined us at a critical moment. Your work has been satisfactory thus far. We need your skills."

Eileen met her gaze with steady resolve. "I'm ready."

"You'll begin immediately. Your task is to manage and verify incoming reports for discrepancies. Accuracy is vital."

Eileen nodded, eager to prove herself.

"Any questions?" asked the Major.

"No, ma'am," Eileen replied.

Lambert motioned to the door. Eileen returned to the room where women bent over typewriters and maps. This room was the centre of real-time intelligence gathering and was receiving top-secret documents daily from all of the intelligence gathering outposts both in England, Europe and overseas.

Privately, Eileen was surprised to be in a new location. "Wasn't I performing well in the supplies room?" she wondered.

The woman in charge was a senior agent and had a reputation for precision. She moved with quiet authority, pointing out the stacks of papers that already awaited Eileen's attention. Eileen settled into her place, aware of the trust being placed in her. The work was relentless but exhilarating, each decoded message a thread in the vast tapestry of war. Her mind traced possibilities, rapidly connecting dots and identifying potential flaws. The hours blurred as Eileen sifted through reports, cross-referenced maps, and flagged anything that seemed out of place. She felt alive with purpose, alive to the stakes that drove everyone in the room. The other women were equally absorbed, shifting only to pore over new maps or pin updates to walls. It was like nothing Eileen had ever experienced—intense, vital, and strangely liberating. Everything was stamped "TOP SECRET."

When the supervisor finally spoke, it startled Eileen from her concentration. "You're surprisingly quick," she said.

In the world outside their busy rooms, the news remained consistently bleak, and Eileen went home each night wondering if Tom was alive and when the war would end.

3

Secret Codes

It turned out that May, 1941, had been one of the coldest springs on record, with snow lying on the hills in the north, and the war still dragging on. By June, however, Eileen realized that the last few nights had not been rocked by bombs. The Blitz, perhaps, was over for now. Soldiers and civilians alike still moved with a weary determination, their faces etched with fatigue, but they slept a bit more soundly.

Coordinating drop-off points for vital supplies became a crucial task, a lifeline amid the chaos. Maps were spread on makeshift tables, marked with hastily drawn routes and strategic locations. Communication crackled over radios, voices urgent yet steady, as plans were made and remade to ensure that the necessary provisions reached their destinations despite the ever-present dangers. The rhythm of this daily struggle was relentless.

Then one day, in September, a note was clipped to one of the supply forms, "Urgent for your eyes only, do not look up or scan the room, look at the *Daily Telegraph* tonight, there will be numbers located in the weather report."

She slid the note into the pocket of her cardigan and kept on with her work. The strangeness of the note buzzed in Eileen's mind as she worked through the day's reports. The hours crept, each tick of the clock a reminder of what she might find.

When she finally reached the flat that evening, Francis and Leslie were out, their absence affording her a rare moment of solitude. She moved quickly, retrieving the *Daily Telegraph* from the sideboard, where Leslie had left it, rather than putting it in the basket by the fire. Her hands trembled slightly as she turned the pages.

She found it, inconspicuous among the weather reports, a string of numbers printed in small, plain type 52002207501. They looked like a compositor's error, but Eileen knew better. It was the same code. Drawing the heavy curtains closed against the dimming light of the evening, Eileen settled at the kitchen table and spread the paper in front of her. She retrieved a small notebook from the sideboard, its pages filled with handwritten letters and numbers, the personal cipher she had constructed.

Her heart raced as she worked through the sequence, each number revealing another piece of the puzzle. The possibilities were dizzying. She scribbled furiously, translating digits into letters, then the numbers started to make sense. They were coordinates. She was curious about where this place might be located, but without any maps at her disposal, she felt at a loss. Her mind raced as she tried to piece together any clues, when suddenly, the door swung open, breaking the silence.

"We're home. How did your day go?" Leslie asked.

"Just the usual," Eileen replied, folding the newspaper and putting it by the fire where it belonged.

The next day, as she worked, she tried to shake off the nagging distraction of the coded message. Reports were piled higher than usual, their contents even more pressing. Eileen pushed thoughts of the code aside and immersed herself in verifying details, aligning maps, and recomposing scrambled words. Her hands moved quickly and efficiently, but her thoughts kept returning to the coordinates.

Her supervisor glanced over once, nodding approval as Eileen flagged a suspicious report for further investigation. Hours passed agonizingly slowly until, finally, the last person had gathered coat and handbag and left the room, signalling the end of another day.

"Goodnight, then," Eileen called out. "I just have one page to finish."

Now was her chance to look at the map and find out where the coordinates pointed. She stood, flexing her cramped fingers, and rolled her shoulders. As she stretched, she scanned the wall where maps of Europe were tacked, their surfaces layered with pins and inked circles.
Acting on impulse, Eileen moved closer, scanning for the location she had decoded. She had to be quick, discreet before the incoming shift noticed her interest. There, her breath caught as she identified a spot: Bletchley, a place rumoured to be at the heart of secret operations. Why was she given these coordinates?

Her thoughts churned as she left for the night. The knowledge must be important, a new mission sparking to life beneath the surface of her daily duties. Back at the flat, Eileen wrestled with why Bletchley had appeared and whether she was right. Why her?

Her sleep was restless, filled with half-formed dreams of codes and maps, and she woke more determined than ever to understand why she was being drawn more deeply into this intrigue.

As weeks passed, Eileen sensed an unspoken tension whenever she entered the Map Room. It was as if someone were watching her more closely. Despite this or perhaps because of it, Eileen redoubled her efforts, working with heightened intensity that mirrored the churning questions in her mind.

Then, in November, another note appeared, slipped subtly among the supply forms. Its presence sent a jolt through Eileen when she saw her name scrawled across the top. She unfolded it with trembling hands: "Well done. Keep watching the weather reports."

Somehow, someone knew she had deciphered the message. Who could have seen her interest in the map that day? She hadn't mentioned it to anyone. Eileen tucked the note away, her thoughts a flurry of anticipation and dread. The coded messages were pulling her into a web of secrets she struggled to understand. Was it safe to pursue this path? And yet, how could she not? The urgency of the war, the ache of Tom's absence, and her own driving need for purpose left her no choice but to follow where the trail led.

That evening, she hurried home, hoping to get there ahead of Leslie and Francis, eager for solitude and discovery. Unfolding the latest *Daily Telegraph*, she scanned the weather reports again. Another line of numbers stared back at her: 3644626224463.

Excitement tempered by caution, she set to work deciphering the new sequence. It came more easily this time, the letters falling into place with an inevitability that quickened her pulse. One of the ways she had learned this technique was to use the letters on the phone dial to transpose the numbers to letters.

"Enigma machine." What was this, and again, why was she chosen to work this out?

The next day, Mitchell stopped her at the entrance to the map room and handed her a sealed envelope. "For you," he said simply, his expression unreadable as he turned away without another word.

Eileen clutched the envelope, her mind racing as she made her way to her desk. She would read it later, away from prying eyes. The Map Room hummed with activity. Reports of U-boat sightings and convoy routes needed immediate attention. Eileen forced herself to concentrate, all the while conscious of the envelope burning a hole in her bag.

As soon as she could slip away unnoticed, Eileen retreated to the narrow restroom down the hall. She locked the door behind her and tore open the envelope with trembling fingers. Inside was a single sheet of paper: "Report at once for urgent reassignment. Full instructions to follow." Beneath it was an address she recognized - Bletchley Park.

She knew that the information they received daily was sometimes almost a day old, and sometimes important details were missed. She was concerned that they, whoever they were, might already know of her involvement, but she also realized that she couldn't ignore this request.

The decision weighed heavily on her as she spent the evening at home, pretending to be engaged in idle conversation with Leslie and Francis. Her mind, however, was miles away, caught between fear and resolve.

The next afternoon, she was handed a train ticket and told to report to Bletchley Park, some 70 miles north of London. When she arrived home that evening, she told Leslie and Francis that the naval office was sending her north on an assignment.

"Will you be gone long?" said Leslie.

"I'm not sure, but I'll keep in touch," she said.

Early the next morning, Eileen found herself standing outside the entrance to Bletchley Park. The imposing mansion loomed against a sky thick with the threat of rain, its shadow casting long doubts she couldn't quite banish. Was this truly where she was meant to be? Were they testing her? Watching for any sign of hesitation?

She showed the guards at the gate her ID, and they escorted her to the main entrance. Steeling herself, Eileen stepped inside, her heart pounding erratically. The air was charged with the same energy that she'd left behind in London. Men and women moved with determined purpose, their whispered conversations hinting at secrets beyond imagining and the importance of what was being asked of her.

She approached a young officer who looked up from his clipboard with careful scrutiny.

"Eileen Green," she announced, trying to keep her voice steady. "I was told to report for reassignment."

The officer nodded, not unfriendly but brisk and efficient. "Follow me," he said, leading her through a labyrinth of hallways that thrummed with activity and into a cramped office lined with filing cabinets.

"Sit tight," he instructed, gesturing to a chair before disappearing back into the bustle.

Minutes stretched into what felt like hours as Eileen waited alone, the tick of a small clock echoing her impatience. She wished for something - anything - to read. Finally, the door swung open, and an older man with thinning hair entered, glancing at her over wire-rimmed spectacles.

"Mrs. Green," he said, the hint of a smile softening his otherwise stern expression. "I'm Lieutenant Arthur Coleman. I've read your file, and we are impressed with your work. We have been investigating you for some time, and it appears that your half brother, Albert Schulte, has been following you and set you up for failure on the buses, only to have you assigned to the Naval Stores division. He is a double agent, and he needed someone he could trust without rousing suspicion. His plan, or its secrecy, has backfired, and we believe you could be instrumental to our operations here. Welcome to Bletchley Park."

Eileen sat in stunned silence, the revelation of her own involvement and the name Schulte, which was her maiden name - her father had changed it to "short" when the war broke out. She could hardly comprehend what the Lieutenant had said. Her ears buzzed as though her head were a staticky radio. This connection was something she had never been aware of, yet suddenly, everything started falling into place like pieces of a puzzle she didn't know was there. Into her memory floated a vague image of Albert among the rescuers who had pulled her out of the wreckage that awful morning. He'd been there one minute and then was gone. What had he been doing there?

Information was passed to the Germans without repercussions. The notes. Enigma. Her mind spun. The man continued, his voice calm and reassuring amidst the turmoil of her thoughts. "You'll find things move quickly here. We need someone with your skills and discretion. The work is demanding but vital."

She nodded, the strangeness of it all pressing heavily but not unpleasantly against her sense of purpose. "What do you need me to do?"

"For now," he said, rising, "acquaint yourself with the team in Block D. They're expecting you, and they've got plenty to keep you busy." As soon as he left the office, Eileen stood on shaky legs, fighting to absorb this strange new world she found herself thrust into. A brother, or half-brother? Could it be true that her own family was tangled up with the enemy? She pushed the questions down, knowing they would have to wait. For now, there was work to be done.

4

The Double Cross

Eileen found Block D, took a deep breath, opened the door and stepped forward, feeling the eyes of the room look up briefly to observe her, but also sensing a camaraderie that echoed what she'd known. Still in a state of shock, she was given a brief tour of the operation. She was assigned a desk and briefed on the daily routine.

She spotted a tea station and headed towards it when Arthur Coleman suddenly approached her and said, "Grab a cup of tea and a biscuit and follow me." Eileen filled a cup with shaking hands and trailed after him, her mind still reeling from the revelations.

"You'll be working with us in Block D," he said over his shoulder, moving quickly down another labyrinthine hallway. "Your background fits precisely with what we're doing."

"And what exactly is that?" she asked, her voice steadier than she felt.

He shot her a quick grin. "You'll see soon enough."

They arrived at a small office crammed with charts and stacks of papers. The man gestured to a chair amidst the chaos.

"Sit," he instructed. Eileen sank into the seat, clutching her tea as though it might steady her thoughts.

"Right," Arthur said, rifling through a heap of documents until he found what he was looking for. "We're on the verge of something big. Your work on the coded messages has already impressed the right people, and your... connections make you uniquely valuable here."

Eileen blinked, forcing herself to focus amidst the whirlwind around her. "So it's true? About my stepbrother?"

Arthur nodded, his expression serious. "We suspect he's been feeding information to the Germans through captured channels. But his connection to you - that complicates things in our favour."

"How did you know?"

"The codes," Arthur replied simply. "Your understanding of them. After some digging, we realized there was more to it than coincidence."

Eileen breathed deeply, absorbing this twist in her life. The thought that she'd been unwittingly linked to enemy operations chilled her, but at the same time, invigorated her resolve. She sipped her tea, determined not to let her hands betray her nerves.

"You never realized that the man on the bus was your stepbrother?" Arthur asked.

"No, I didn't," she answered, "and I don't remember anyone in the family ever talking about him." Arthur's face softened with understanding.

"It's a lot to take in. But here, you can turn it to our advantage." Eileen nodded slowly, the shock still blooming within her. "What do you need me to do?"

"We're working on a large-scale deception operation," Arthur said, his voice urgent yet steady.

"The goal is to feed Schulte, your stepbrother, carefully crafted information. We think you can help make it believable."

The difficulty of the plan struck her, but she felt an inner resolve harden like steel.

"I'll do everything I can."

Arthur smiled with a hint of admiration. "I had a feeling you'd say that. Come, let's get you started."

He led her through more crowded rooms and into a smaller section where tension ran high. Eileen could sense the critical nature of their mission, the immense stakes for which they laboured day and night. They handed her stacks of coded messages, and she immersed herself, losing track of time amid the intricate web of numbers and letters. Slowly, the chatter around her faded into a distant hum.

When she finally looked up, hours had passed, and the room was bustling with even more frenetic energy. Arthur appeared again, this time carrying a roll of maps under his arm.

"How are you getting on?" he asked. Eileen rubbed her eyes and managed a determined smile.

"I'm beginning to see patterns."

"Excellent," Arthur replied, glancing over her work. "We need those insights to build our next move."

He unrolled the maps across a table and motioned for her to join him in examining them. Eileen stood beside him, studying the lines and markings that crisscrossed the paper in a dizzying array of possibilities.

"This is where we need your skills," Arthur said, tapping a location marked with several question marks. "We can't afford any mistakes." Eileen leaned in, her mind racing as she connected the dots between the maps and messages. She could feel Arthur's confidence in her abilities - a silent yet powerful encouragement.

"I think," she said slowly, "I see how we can lead him toward this site without compromising our real operations."

Arthur watched her closely, nodding with approval. "Go on."

"If we synchronize these transmissions," Eileen continued, pointing to the coded messages stacked next to the maps, "and scatter them with plausible movements, it might just be enough to convince him."

"And you think Schulte will take the bait?"

Eileen hesitated only a moment before answering. "If he thinks I'm involved, he won't suspect a thing."

Arthur's eyes sparked with admiration again. "Exactly what we need. Your intuition on this is invaluable."

She returned to her desk with renewed focus, the earlier shock of revelation now transformed into an unwavering commitment. Her hands no longer trembled as she sorted through the codes, her mind mapping out the intricate deceptions with precision and clarity. She was, however, very glad that her father was not in London. She wouldn't have known how to face him.

The following days saw Eileen deeply entrenched in the operation, her confidence growing with each successful transmission they orchestrated. Her world had narrowed to this mission, and everything else seemed a pale echo. Arthur checked on her often, his faith in her both grounding and inspiring. She was surprised at how easily they worked together, their strategies aligning seamlessly as they advanced the plan.

"Mrs. Green," Arthur called one afternoon, waving her over to his crowded corner of the office. "Up for another challenge?"

She joined him, eager for what came next.

"This is a bit more involved," he said, handing her a thick bundle of documents. "We need these decoded and ready by tomorrow. It's critical for our next move."

Eileen took the stack, her eyes scanning the columns of numbers and letters. "I'll see to it," she promised, already diving into the complex sequences on the top page.

"Good," Arthur replied, satisfied. "You're doing brilliantly. Just remember to breathe occasionally."

She managed a small laugh, feeling the camaraderie of his words. Long after most of the others had left for the night, Eileen remained at her desk, illuminated by a single lamp in the hushed office. Her earlier doubts had melted away, replaced by a fierce dedication to their cause.

The next morning dawned with grey skies and an urgency that outpaced even the day before. Eileen delivered the decoded messages straight to Arthur, who barely glanced at them before nodding appreciatively.

"Perfect," he said, handing them off to another agent. "Now let's see how Albert Schulte reacts."

They waited tensely for hours, monitoring each transmission with meticulous care. When confirmation finally arrived that their planted information had been passed along, the room erupted with a rare cheer. Eileen felt a thrill of victory surge through her, a vindication of her efforts and sacrifices.

Arthur approached her amidst the subdued celebration, his expression one of satisfaction mingled with something deeper. "You've outdone yourself," he said. "The success of this phase is largely thanks to you."

Eileen shook her head modestly, though she couldn't suppress a smile. "I just followed your plan."

"And improved it," Arthur countered, his gaze steady. "We couldn't have done this without you." She absorbed his words, feeling the weight of their truth settle over her like an honour and a burden alike. It was the validation she'd craved since Tom's absence left her searching for purpose, but it also reminded her of the precarious line they walked.

"What's next?" she asked, eager to channel her momentum into further action.

He handed her another set of documents with a slightly more relaxed air. "Let's keep the momentum going."

Eileen took them, feeling more a part of this world with each passing moment. The seriousness of their deception plan no longer intimidated her; it spurred her to push further, dig deeper, and outwit even the most cunning operatives.

As days turned into weeks, she was occasionally able to return home to her brother's. At the end of 1941 she was able to spend a couple of days off with her family for Christmas but had to make up lots of stories about why she was not working at Whitehall. Her analytical mind thrived in this environment of constant challenge and danger. She moved with purpose, each task building upon the last.

Lieutenant Arthur Coleman was a constant presence, his subtle encouragement never wavering.

"You're becoming quite the natural," he remarked one evening as they reviewed another set of decoded messages.

"Desperation is a good motivator," Eileen replied, only half in jest.

Arthur nodded, understanding her unspoken fears and hopes. "It's more than that," he said. "You've found something you're meant to do."

His words lingered with her, even as the demands of their work filled every waking moment. She no longer felt like an outsider in this world of secrets and shadows; instead, she was at its very heart, guiding the treacherous currents with deft precision.

One morning in February 1942, he handed her a note, its edges slightly worn and its paper crisp to the touch. As Eileen unfolded it, she discovered a series of strange, cryptic symbols scattered across the page. Her mind flickered back to a distant memory of her history class in school, where she had encountered something vaguely similar. "This is completely out of the ordinary," she remarked, her voice tinged with intrigue and a hint of anxiety. "Where did it come from?"

"We intercepted it from Albert during an encounter with another agent in the field. We believe it is from northern Scotland.

Could you investigate any potential links to the Nazi regime and their interest in cryptic symbols?"

"I'll do my best," Eileen responded, "but I have no idea what the symbols might mean. I may need to use the British Library for a few days."

"There is a small library in the main house. Perhaps you could look there first."

That evening, she ventured beyond the huts where she had spent her time and searched the large house at the heart of Bletchley Park in search of the library and a book that might provide some insight.

As she scanned the shelves, Eileen's fingers brushed against a promising volume: *Ancient Runes and Their Modern Uses*. Tucking it under her arm, she returned to her desk in Block D and immersed herself in its pages. The symbols on the note began to take on new meaning, connecting in unexpected ways to the coded messages she'd been intercepting.

She worked late into the night, piecing together what felt like a separate puzzle within their broader operation, her exhaustion overshadowed by the intrigue of this new discovery. Finally, as dawn broke over Bletchley Park, she set down her pen, excitement mingling with dread over what the breakthrough might reveal.

When Eileen presented her findings to Arthur Coleman, his eyes widened in astonishment. "An occult connection," he murmured. "Hitler's fixation with mysticism. This could be more significant than we realized."

Eileen nodded. "If Albert's involved, it suggests they're exploring other angles."

5

In search of a Cryptic Connection

Eileen stood on the platform of a soot-covered train station, in the small village of Rosslyn in Scotland, seven miles from Edinburgh, clutching her suitcase and watching steam curl upwards like spectral fingers. She was alone, having been sent to Scotland at Arthur's insistence to follow the trail opened by the cryptic symbols. He'd assured her it was essential and she was the only one who could piece it together.

Nevertheless, being abruptly separated from the team left her feeling unsettled. Her journey north had been long. The train wheezed into life again, leaving behind a silence broken only by the echo of boots on wet cobblestones as a uniformed man approached through the mist.

"Mrs. Green?" he said, "I'm glad to see you arrived safely."

"Yes," she replied, adjusting her grip on the suitcase. "I'm surprised to see you Mr. Mitchell."

"I'm actually John Mitchell, MI5," he smiled and extended his hand. "I've been assigned to assist you here."

The tension in her chest eased slightly. She shook his hand. "Thank you. Any local contacts we can trust?"

John nodded, his expression serious. "We've identified a few, but we need to proceed cautiously. People here are suspicious by nature."

"Understood," Eileen replied, aware of the delicacy required in her task.

They walked through the grey streets to the Rosslyn Inn. Eileen settled into her small room, suddenly grateful for the brief respite from her duties in London and Bletchley. As she unpacked, she felt the pull of uncertainty - how deep did this new conspiracy run, and how far would it lead her from everything familiar? Her thoughts were interrupted by a knock at the door.

John stood there, his presence steadying. "Up for a walk?" he asked. "It might help us get our bearings."

Eileen agreed, putting on her trench coat and gloves. They ventured back into the misty streets. The town was small, with its buildings huddled against the persistent chill of the northern air. At the other end of town, they found a local pub and ordered at the bar, amidst the low murmur of voices and the clinking of glasses. The warmth and noise were a welcome contrast to the solitude of her room.

Over a pint of ale, John briefed her on their situation. "There's been unusual radio activity linked to these symbols," he said, keeping his voice low. "Locals whisper about strange gatherings in the hills."

Eileen listened intently, her analytical mind sifting through each piece of information. "We need to establish where and when those gatherings are happening," she said.

John nodded, his eyes scanning the room cautiously. "There's an old historian in town who might know more, but he's wary of outsiders."

"Think he'll talk to us?"

"If we tread carefully," John replied, leaning back with a hint of a smile. "And if you charm him as you do Lieutenant Coleman."

46

Eileen flushed slightly but met his teasing with a determined look. "I'll do what's needed."

They stayed until closing, then began their journey back to the inn. As they walked through the dimly lit streets, Eileen suddenly noticed something. "Look," she exclaimed, her eyes focused on a garden wall. The moonlight illuminated a weathered symbol, intricately carved into the stone and covered in moss, accompanied by an arrow pointing the way. John, puzzled, remarked that he had travelled this road a few times and had never noticed the mysterious marking.

Eileen's pulse quickened, her mind racing with possibilities. "We're closer than we thought," she said.

John studied the symbol, an edge creeping into his voice. "Let's head back and revisit this in the morning."

Eileen nodded. "We need to follow this lead before it goes cold." She sketched the symbol in her notebook, knowing it might connect back to the notes they'd seen at Bletchley Park.

The next day, after little sleep, they met for breakfast in the dining room, pretending to be a couple visiting from London. Her eyes lingered on the other patrons, assessing each one for signs of undue interest in their presence. Satisfied they weren't being watched, Eileen turned her attention back to John.

After breakfast, they set out to find the village historian. John knew his name was Angus Hines, and he lived in town. Eileen was determined to extract any clues about the gatherings rumoured to involve Nazi sympathizers or those swayed by their occult beliefs.

"How should we approach him?" she asked.

He considered this for a moment. "Angus is likely to be skeptical," John replied. "We'll need to win his trust. If we can convince him we're not a threat, he might be willing to help." They made their way to his residence, a small and unassuming building. They knocked on the door, and an older man, his face lined with suspicion, opened the door.

"Mr. Hines?" John began cautiously.

"Yes, and who might you two be?" Angus said with suspicion.

"We are from London - connected to Naval Intelligence - and we were hoping you might answer a few questions."

"I don't care much for company," Angus replied without looking at them directly, keeping them from entering. "What questions could you possibly have for an old man in a tiny Scottish village?"

"We have encountered some ancient symbols, and they may be associated with specific activities in the area. I was told that you are the local historian."

"I might know a thing or two," he said, cautiously looking around. "Activities, you say?" Angus's gruff voice took on a note of curiosity. "You'd best be clear about your intent. People round here don't fancy outsiders poking their noses in. Come off the street then."

John stepped forward. "We understand your hesitation, Mr. Hines. But we believe there are dangerous elements at play, and we're trying to prevent harm."

Angus studied them for a long moment, then nodded sharply as though deciding something.

"Well then," he said, his tone grudgingly cooperative. "Best come through to the back where we can speak."

Eileen exchanged a quick glance with John, relieved they had passed this first hurdle. They followed Angus into a cluttered back room stacked with crates of books and old maps. He motioned for them to sit at an uneven table as he settled across from them.

"So," Angus said, rubbing his chin thoughtfully. "You're asking about symbols?"

Eileen opened her notebook, showing him the sketch of the symbol they'd found on the wall. "This one in particular," she said, watching his reaction closely.

Angus's eyes lingered on the drawing, and she noticed a flicker of recognition before he masked it with a shrug. "Aye, that's an old cove marking," he said. "Smugglers used them up and down these parts."

Eileen leaned forward with interest. "But why would they be showing up now?"

"People find use for old things when times get desperate," Angus replied cryptically.

"And what about the gatherings in the hills?" John pressed gently. "We've heard talk."

Angus frowned, his expression guarded again. "More than talk, I'm thinking," he muttered, then sighed as though surrendering to a truth he'd rather not face. "There have been meetings. Folks drawn into ideas best left alone."

Eileen felt a chill at his words. "Do you know where they're happening?"

Angus paused for a moment, then stood up, opened a pantry door, and retrieved three shot glasses and a bottle of Scotland's finest whisky. "I need to know why you might be curious before I continue," he said.

John looked at Eileen and carefully chose his words. "As I said before, we are with Naval Intelligence," he admitted, his voice steady and direct. "We've seen these symbols before, linked to Nazi operations."

Angus poured the whisky, his expression hardening. Eileen accepted the drink, sensing the importance of this moment. "You think there's Germans mixed up in this?" Angus asked, his skepticism tinged with concern.

"We don't know yet," Eileen said. "That's why we're here."

Angus took a sip from his glass and leaned back, considering them anew. For a moment, the room was filled only with the quiet ticking of a clock on the wall.

"There was a fellow in town asking about a diagram or map a couple of weeks ago. He said he was a reporter up here from London investigating a rumour of an invasion scare. Maybe it was just talk to cover his real intent." Angus's voice lowered, as if the walls themselves might betray him. "Some think he might've been a German agent, and he's not the only one."

"Did you get a name?" Eileen asked.

"Called himself Charles," Angus replied. "But I didn't believe him, too shifty for my liking."

John looked at Eileen, both aware that this lead could be crucial. "And the gatherings," John prompted. "Can you tell us where?"

Angus hesitated, then stood and rummaged through stacks of papers. He returned with an old hand-drawn map, laying it on the table. "The cove markings point to places like these," he said, indicating several spots circled in pencil. "All up in the hills, places no one but locals would know about."

"Would you know anyone who could guide us?" John asked.

Angus's eyes narrowed slightly, gauging their resolve. "Might," he said. "But if you're followed - if you're caught - it won't just be your necks in the noose."

"We understand the risk," Eileen said firmly.

Angus studied them for another moment, then nodded. "Young lad named Finlay. Knows the hills better than his own boots. I'll have him meet you at dawn tomorrow, if you're sure."

"We're sure," John confirmed.

Eileen traced her finger over the map, her mind already plotting their next move. "This is exactly what we needed," she said quietly, her gratitude evident.

Angus leaned back with a wary sigh. "You'll need it and more," he muttered. "There's talk of something big happening soon. Don't know what or when, but folks are on edge."

John pocketed the map carefully, aware of its significance. "We appreciate your help, Mr. Hines."

6

A Journey into the Mystic

The sky was still grey with the promise of dawn as Eileen and John set off, the chill of the morning seeping through their coats. They moved quickly, eager to leave town behind before curious eyes could follow. Finlay, a wiry youth with wind-chapped cheeks and a cautious demeanour, joined them at the edge of the village where the road gave way to a rugged path into the hills.

"Hope you've got good boots," he said by way of greeting, eyeing Eileen and John with a mix of skepticism and curiosity.

John nodded. "You're certain about this route?"

"Certain as rain in Scotland," Finlay replied, leading them up a narrow trail that twisted through the heathered landscape. His movements were quick and sure-footed, even as mist curled around their ankles like something alive.

Eileen kept pace, her mind racing with possibilities. She replayed Angus's warnings in her head. They were venturing into dangerous territory, led by clues as elusive as the morning fog. Each step took them further from safety and deeper into uncertainty.

They walked in silence for a time, only the distant call of a bird breaking the stillness. Eileen felt a mounting tension, the importance of their task weighing heavily. She glanced at John, whose steady presence brought some comfort.

"How far to the first location?" John asked as they paused to catch their breath on a rocky incline.

Finlay pointed ahead with a measured nod. "Just over that ridge," he said. "But be careful. Ancient ruins up there. Place has eyes."

Eileen exchanged a look with John, understanding the implications. They were likely being watched even now, their every move calculated by those who might wish them harm.

"Thank you," she said to Finlay, her voice carrying both determination and caution.

They pressed on, the landscape growing ever more desolate. The ruins came into view - a cluster of stone remnants against the bleak horizon. Eileen felt a shiver, knowing how exposed they were.

Finlay hung back, his gaze scanning the area with practised vigilance. "I'll keep a lookout," he said, watching them approach the site.

Eileen and John crept forward, their senses alert. Every crunch of gravel beneath their feet echoed like a warning. They exchanged a silent nod before stepping into the shelter of the crumbling walls.

Inside, Eileen's eyes darted over the stone surfaces. "Here," she whispered urgently, pointing to a fresh set of markings etched into the wall. They matched those in her notebook, a confirmation, yet raising more questions than answers.

John studied them grimly. "They're using this place all right," he said. "But for what?"

The sound of distant voices cut through the air.
"Quick!"

They ducked behind a low stone wall as the voices grew nearer. Eileen's heart pounded, her mind racing through possible escape routes. John glanced over the edge, assessing the threat.

54

"Could be a decoy to flush us out," he muttered, tension in every syllable.

Eileen nodded, crouching lower. "Or someone's tipped them off."

The voices multiplied, closer now, a jumble of urgent tones carried on the wind. Eileen strained to hear, catching fragments that sent a chill through her. Words in German and English with a distinct Scots accent - disjointed but unmistakable. They seemed to be searching for something; then one of them started to speak English.

He said, "I think the symbols are over here."

All of a sudden a gunshot rang out, "Who'd be trespassing on my land?" Then there was the sound of running towards the south hill.

"What are we going to do?" whispered Eileen. Finlay stood and waved.

"Is that you, Finlay?"

"Yes, Callum."

"What the hell are you doing up here, laddie? You know there's been some disturbances lately; you could have been hurt."

Then Eileen and John appeared from behind the wall, dusting themselves off with a mix of embarrassment and relief.

"We weren't expecting company," John said, his tone a careful mix of apology and authority.

Callum squinted at them suspiciously, lowering the rifle. "And who might you two be?"

"They're with me," Finlay interjected quickly. "From London."

"And why would you be roaming around these parts?" Callum said.

John continued, "We are with Naval Intelligence, and we have reason to believe the Nazis have an interest in the area, but we have yet to determine why."

Eileen nodded, stepping forward to defuse the tension. "We didn't mean to intrude, if this is your property. We're just investigating some unsettling news."

Callum's gaze shifted between them, his wariness evident. "Angus sent word this morning," he said finally. "Said you might be around."

"You gave us quite a scare," Eileen confessed, her voice steady despite the adrenaline still coursing through her.

"Was about to say the same," Callum replied, though the hint of a grin betrayed his humour. He looked over his shoulder to make sure the others were gone, then turned back with renewed focus. "Angus said you're looking for symbols?"

"Yes, we are."

Callum nodded, handing the rifle to Finlay before motioning them towards another nearby ruin. "This way," he said, leading them to an area partially hidden by overgrown brush.

As they ducked inside, Eileen's eyes widened with realization. More markings adorned the walls, intricate and deliberate.

"It's all connected," she murmured, tracing the lines with her finger.

Callum observed her intently, his eyes reflecting a deep curiosity. "These artifacts date back to ancient times," he said, gesturing towards the weathered relics. "They've been here for hundreds of years." His voice carried a sense of awe and reverence for the history embodied in the walls before them.

"Do you know what they mean?" John inquired, his tone revealing a casual indifference.

"I've never really paid much attention to them. Angus might," Callum replied thoughtfully. "And if he doesn't have the answers, he probably knows someone who does."

John took in the scene, his expression one of grim determination. "We need to document this," he said. "Every detail."

Eileen pulled out her notebook, sketching quickly as John surveyed the area for anything they might have missed. The markings were fresh, suggesting ongoing activity - something bigger than they had anticipated.

"Will you help us?" Eileen asked Callum, looking up from her work.

Callum hesitated, then nodded slowly. "Aye. But if you're found out - if any harm comes to my people - I'll end this quick."

Eileen met his gaze unflinchingly. "We won't let that happen. We'll ensure your safety."

Eileen and John continued to look around at the ancient ruins, taking in as much as they could in the time allotted.

"I suggest you hurry before someone else shows up. Finlay can guide you back to the village," Callum offered, his tone shifting to one of cautious alliance.

Eileen thanked him. She made diagrams as quickly as she could before they headed back. Finlay waited outside, restless but patient.

"We'll get these to Angus," John said. "See what he can make of them."

"Mind yourselves," Callum warned. "Others might not scare as easily as this lot."

Eileen nodded, aware of the stakes and buoyed by the new information. Callum's help had given them an edge, but they were far from secure.

As they departed, leaving Callum behind in the growing darkness, Eileen felt a renewed sense of purpose. They moved quickly back to town.

Angus was at the bar of the inn, and his face reflected a mix of relief and impatience when he saw them.

"It's getting riskier every day," he said as they entered. "What did you find?"

Eileen handed him the notebook, her fingers brushing against the worn leather cover. "We documented everything," she replied, her voice filled with both exhaustion and resolve.

Angus flipped through the pages, his eyes narrowing as he absorbed the information. "This confirms it," he muttered, almost to himself.

Eileen exchanged a glance with John, both sensing the gravity of Angus's reaction. "Confirms what?" she pressed.

"That you're not the only ones after this," Angus said grimly, setting the notebook down on a scarred wooden table. "It's bigger than we thought, bigger than even MI5 might realize." "Come to my home in the morning. I have some old books and diagrams that look very similar to these symbols."

Eileen's heart leapt at the prospect. "You think they might help us understand more?"

Angus nodded, though his expression remained grim. "Aye. But it also means whoever's using them knows a damn sight more than we do."

John leaned over the table, his jaw set with determination. "We'll need to move fast, then. We can't risk losing our advantage."

The weight of his words pressed on Eileen as she considered the implications. Their mission, once a small piece in the grand scheme of war, now seemed to connect to something vast and treacherous. She was both terrified and exhilarated by the scope of it.

"We'll be there first thing," she promised Angus, her voice steady.

They both sat back and had some dinner by the fire, discussing the day's events. Then retired.

The next day, they arrived at Angus's home and found the door open. Cautiously, they entered and called out, at last finding Angus lying in the back room, dazed and confused. "Angus, what happened here?" John asked, rushing to his side.

"Didn't see them," Angus muttered, struggling to sit up. "Came from nowhere - two men. Ransacked the place."

Eileen's eyes darted around the cluttered room, taking in the overturned shelves and scattered papers. Her heart sank as she noticed a conspicuous gap where the books must have been. "They took everything?" she asked, helping steady Angus.

"Not all. I'd hidden some of it," Angus replied with a wry grin. "Too old to be outsmarted completely."

John exhaled sharply, relief mixed with frustration. "Did you recognize them?" Angus shook his head, wincing.

"Strangers to me. Knew what they were after, though. Didn't take much else."

Eileen glanced at John, her mind racing with possibilities. "They must be getting desperate," she said, her voice urgent. "If they're this close..."

John nodded grimly.

Angus got up and Eileen put the kettle on to make some tea." What did they take?" she asked.

Angus composed himself and said, "Rosicrucians. They were looking for a manuscript on the secret order of the Rosicrucians, but they didn't find it."

Eileen asked with curiosity, "Who are the Rosicrucians?"

Angus poured the tea, his movements steadying as he spoke. "An old society, shrouded in mystery. Some say they hold secrets from ancient Egypt and beyond, knowledge that could change the world, or destroy it."

Eileen absorbed this, her thoughts aligning with the symbols they'd found. "And how does it connect to us?"

"That's what those men wanted to find out," Angus said darkly. "But I doubt they know how deep it runs."

Angus reached under a pile of disordered papers, pulling out several yellowed documents and a faded diagram. "They didn't find these," he said with satisfaction.

Eileen took them, her hands trembling slightly with the weight of their significance. Each paper felt like a piece of a vast, intricate puzzle. "Are there others looking for these?" she asked, trying to gauge the danger.

"Aye," Angus replied, rubbing his head where a bruise was forming. "Those two were just the start. You'd best watch yourselves."

John inspected the papers closely. The symbols and diagrams mirrored those in Eileen's notebook, their meanings still elusive yet undeniably vital.

"We need to take these back to Bletchley Park," he said, urgency in his voice.

"And what about you?" Eileen looked at Angus with concern. "It's not safe for you here anymore."

"Don't worry about me," Angus said sharply, though his eyes softened at her concern. "I've been dodging trouble longer than you've been alive. Just make sure you uncover whatever they're after before they do."

The resolve in his words bolstered Eileen's own determination. She tucked the documents securely into her leather satchel, turned to Angus and, to his surprise, hugged him and said, "We owe you more than we can say."

Angus patted her back gruffly. "Just get the bastards."

They left Angus, knowing that time was now their greatest enemy. Each step seemed to echo with the dangers that lay ahead; yet beneath it all was a quiet thrill at being so close to unlocking what others had tried to keep hidden. They moved quickly through the village, aware of every passerby and shadow that might conceal another threat. Between them, the documents felt like living things, pulsing with history and danger.

Back at the inn, they wasted no time. John spread the papers across the table in his room, matching them against the notes from their previous informants. Eileen watched as he worked, his focus intense and unyielding. She sensed a shift in him, a recognition of the size of what they had stumbled upon.

"This changes everything," John said finally, looking up from the intricate web of symbols. "If these societies are connected..."

"It could mean they've been operating under your noses, our noses, for years," Eileen finished, her voice filled with awe and apprehension.

They both knew the implications were staggering. What began as a lead on possible German sympathizers now extended into layers of conspiracy that spanned centuries. And they were at the centre of it.

"We need to get this to someone we can trust," John said. "If they're watching Angus, they might be onto us sooner than we think."

Eileen nodded, already formulating a plan in her mind. "Lieutenant Coleman," she said decisively. "He's sharp enough to help us sort through this without drawing too much attention."
"I think Angus is concealing something else," she added.

"Maybe. If so, we need to uncover what that is," John replied.

Eileen stared at the papers. "If we don't get ahead of this, it could be catastrophic."

They exchanged looks.

"Let's go back as soon as it's dark," John said. "We can hope whoever assaulted Angus has gone up into the hills."

They left the inn after a late tea, the streets silent and dark. Their breaths came out in cold puffs as they navigated through shadowed alleys. They reached his house and knocked on the door. Angus answered. His expression was one of mingled relief and surprise at their return.
"You're back quicker than I thought," he said, ushering them inside. "Didn't expect to see you until morning."

John wasted no time. "You hinted there was something more. We need it now."

Angus nodded, a glint of understanding in his eyes. "Figured you'd come sniffing for it." He led them to a heavy wooden chest in the corner, its surface scarred and ancient-looking.

"Help me with this?" Angus asked, motioning to John. Together, they dragged the chest into the light. Its hinges creaked as Angus opened it, revealing a jumble of old books and a rolled parchment.

"This is what they wanted," Angus said, handing it to Eileen. He carefully unrolled the parchment and placed a heavy weight on each corner to keep it flat. The material was brittle, and the ink faded, but still readable. Eileen leaned in, her breath catching as she realized what they were seeing.

"Is it a map?" John said, astonishment in his voice.

A map or a diagram, but unlike any she'd ever seen. It was filled with strange symbols and annotations, each line and marking suggesting an ancient purpose, pathways known only to the initiated. Eileen's mind raced to connect it with the other papers they had, envisioning how it could all fit together.

"This is why they're after you," she said to Angus. "This connects everything."

Angus nodded grimly. "The bastards think it'll lead them to more - something bigger than what they've got so far."

John exchanged a tense glance with Eileen. "Then we can't let them have it."

She carefully re-rolled the parchment and tucked it securely away with the other documents. Every second felt precious now, each moment potentially leading to another encounter. "We need to get back to Bletchley as soon as possible."

They started out early the next morning. The train station was bathed in the pale light of dawn when Eileen and John arrived, their senses alert for any sign they were being followed. They boarded the train quickly, settling into a compartment near the back where they could watch for anyone showing undue interest.

As the train pulled away from the platform, Eileen felt a knot in her chest begin to ease. She glanced at John, whose expression mirrored her own mix of exhaustion and determination.

"We need to be ready," he said quietly, as if even the walls might listen.

Eileen nodded. "Do you think there are others on this route?" she asked.

John's eyes were sharp and calculating. "It certainly seems so," he replied. "But we've got the advantage now."

The return journey was tense, the weight of their discovery pressing heavily upon them. The landscape rushed past in a blur of grey and green as they headed south, each mile drawing them closer to Bletchley Park and the answers they sought.

7

Hidden Connections

Back at Bletchley Park, Eileen and John wasted no time. They moved quickly through the maze of corridors, searching for Arthur Coleman, who looked up from his desk, surprised and concerned as they entered. "You're back sooner than expected," he said, taking in their travel-worn appearance.

"We found more than we bargained for," John replied, laying the satchel on Arthur's desk, looking worried.

Eileen unrolled the parchment, the ancient diagram spreading out like a revelation.

"There were others searching in Rosslyn. We think this was their target," she said.

Arthur's eyes widened as he examined it. "Incredible," he murmured. "If these symbols are what I think they are..."

"They're connected to something much larger," Eileen interjected. "It changes everything we thought we knew," Eileen finished, her voice urgent.

They took more than an hour telling him what had happened and explaining their conversation with Angus.

"Thank you. Leave it with me. It may take me a few days to organize our next steps. Carry on," said Arthur.

On the next Monday Arthur left word for Eileen to report to him when she arrived at her desk. When she arrived at his office, his secretary led her through a long corridor to a room little more than a storage area. Three tables had been set up, and Arthur and John were waiting. There were two others also ahead of her. Like Eileen, they were analysts: he'd chosen them for their expertise in history and physics as well as their skill with code-breaking.

He laid out the scope of their findings. "This goes beyond just a code-breaking operation," he announced. "We're dealing with something larger, something that could shift the balance of power."

Eileen watched the faces around her, some filled with disbelief, others with determination. They worked, piecing together the hidden connections that spanned continents and centuries. As more details came to light, the complexity of the conspiracy grew ever more staggering.

"We need to move fast," John added, his voice cutting through the charged atmosphere. "If they suspect we know what they are looking for..."

The room buzzed as plans were made and roles assigned. Eileen found herself at the centre of it all; her analytical skills and newfound knowledge made her indispensable.

Arthur pulled her aside as the meeting concluded. "You're key to this," he said, his voice both reassuring and insistent. "We couldn't have progressed this far without you."

Eileen nodded, feeling the weight of his words. "Where do you need me?"

"Whitehall is where you're needed most now. We need to continue the deception while we work on this new information." Arthur replied. "But keep your comings and goings discreet."

Eileen understood, and she prepared to divide her time between London and Bletchley, aware of the dangers in both places as she shuttled back and forth, carrying the latest intelligence and coded instructions. Her world shrank to the relentless pursuit of answers that could change the course of the war. Each trip was tense. It felt as though London had been transformed. The streets were shrouded in darkness when she went to work and when she returned home in the evening, with only the moon and stars providing a faint glow. Air raid sirens still wailed from time to time like mournful ghosts, sending citizens scurrying to shelters. The city felt alive with secrets and whispers, every corner hiding potential spies or informants.

At Bletchley, the team worked around the clock, studying the diagrams and papers Eileen and John had brought back from Scotland, decoding and analyzing. Every new piece of information drew them deeper into the labyrinth, revealing layers of deception and intrigue that stretched even beyond what they'd imagined. In London, Eileen maintained her cover at Naval Stores, careful not to arouse suspicion as she gathered updates from Arthur.

Then, among one of the daily reports, a note stood out, its presence marked by an unusual symbol etched in the top right corner. This note was definitely not part of the standard package. Eileen scanned the room, her gaze lingering momentarily on each of her colleagues, gauging their reactions.

The message was cryptic, filled with a jumble of letters and numbers, but Eileen recognized it as a personal cipher. Her mind raced through the possibilities: could this be Albert's doing, or was it something new, a trap set by those who suspected her involvement?

The uncertainty gnawed at her. She knew she had to decode it quickly, but without drawing attention. Eileen tucked the note into her pocket, forcing herself to remain calm and focused as she completed the day's tasks.

That evening, back at the London flat, she spread the note out on the table. Leslie and Francis were out for the night, leaving her alone with her thoughts and suspicions. She translated the code into something coherent, but it was the strange symbol that had her thinking. She sat back. Was this another clue to the diagram they had found?

She needed to confide in Arthur, whose strategic mind was best equipped to handle such a threat. He had said to return to Bletchley should she discover something new, instructing her in that case to take the train in the morning as if it were a normal day.

8

The Turning Point

E ileen followed Arthur's instructions carefully, maintaining a facade of calm and routine as she prepared to leave London. Saying goodbye to Francis, she left the flat, the envelope with the cryptic note tucked securely in her bag. The streets were bustling with morning activity, and she moved quickly, blending with the crowd.

She reached the station and boarded the train, choosing a compartment near the rear where she could watch for anyone taking undue interest in her movements. Every passenger seemed an agent of fate, another potential threat.

At Bletchley Park, Arthur was surprised to see her. "What has happened?" he asked, dispensing with formalities. Eileen nodded, handing him the envelope.

"I believe it's linked to Albert because a well-dressed individual exited the room right after I found it."

"What makes you think he's involved?" Arthur asked curiously.

"Look at the symbol and the writing. It looks very familiar, and the cryptic symbols are like the diagram we have."

At that moment, there was a knock on the door. "Come in," Arthur said.

"Sorry to disturb you, sir, but we've found something in the diagram that you need to see."

Eileen and Arthur followed the young historian through the maze of corridors until they reached their room. The tables were covered with maps and coded documents. Eileen recognized some of the papers they had brought from Rosslyn. Everyone looked up as they entered, anticipation lighting their faces.

"Show us what you've got," Arthur said.

The analyst stepped forward, pointing to the ancient diagram Eileen and John had recovered. "When you brought this in, we started cross-referencing it with everything we've intercepted so far," he said. "The symbols match those used in earlier transmissions, which we've noticed for months, ones we thought were dead leads."

Eileen felt a jolt of recognition. "But they're not," she said, her mind racing ahead. "They're part of a larger network."

The analyst nodded, excited. "Exactly. We've pieced together enough to suggest these societies, the Rosicrucian and others, are more organized than anyone thought. We have encountered several dead ends in our quest, but there is hope. I met a distinguished professor at the University of Edinburgh while I was studying there, James Beattie, who is a celebrated cryptographer, and might offer the expertise we need. His insights could provide the breakthrough we're seeking. I took the liberty of contacting him and making arrangements for his arrival. I hope that's alright. He will be joining us tomorrow, albeit late in the evening, ready to lend his considerable knowledge to our cause."

"Great job, everyone," Arthur said. "I'm eager to meet him. In the meantime, let's get back to work." The analysts returned to their tasks, the room buzzing with renewed focus. Arthur gestured for Eileen to follow him back to his office.

"You were right," he said, handing her back the decoded note. "This is larger than we imagined. Go home and get some rest; we'll need you sharp when Beattie arrives."

Eileen nodded, but rest felt impossible. The pieces were aligning too perfectly, yet shadows of doubt loomed large. She left Arthur and returned to London.

Leslie was in the kitchen, tinkering with a small radio when she walked in. "You're back early," he commented, glancing up.

Eileen forced a casual tone. "Quiet day at the office," she said, setting her bag down carefully.

Francis appeared from the bedroom, her eyes bright with curiosity. "Anything exciting happening?"

"Not much," Eileen replied, knowing they sensed more than she let on. "The usual paperwork."

Leslie shook his head, amused. "You don't fool us," he said lightly. "We know you're doing more than that."

Eileen smiled, grateful for their support despite the secrets she had to keep. But even as they settled into dinner and conversation, her thoughts were miles away, caught in the intricate web she now found herself enmeshed in. Sleep came fitfully, dreams filled with coded messages and shifting alliances. When Eileen woke, her urge to be useful propelled her back to Bletchley Park before noon.

The day passed in a blur of anticipation and preparation for Professor Beattie's arrival. Eileen worked alongside the analysts to organize and compile all the information they'd gathered, ensuring every lead was ready to be examined with fresh eyes.
An air of expectancy settled over their little corner of Block D. The analysts were aware that this could be a turning point in their mission.

Eileen reviewed her notes, the minutes stretching into hours. The weight of their discoveries loomed large, and she felt its press even in the charged silence. It was well past dark when a commotion at the entrance signalled Beattie's arrival. Eileen looked up from her desk as a distinguished figure appeared, flanked by Arthur and John Mitchell. Professor Beattie carried himself with an air of refined authority, his hair gleaming under the harsh lights. Eileen stood to one side, observing as Beattie took in the flurry of activity around him.

"Quite an operation you have here," he remarked, his voice carrying the hint of a Scottish lilt.

Arthur nodded. "We're hoping your expertise can shed light on some rather unusual findings," he said, gesturing to the spread of documents and diagrams.

Beattie's eyes settled on the ancient parchment first, his expression sharpening with interest.

"Fascinating," he murmured, tracing a finger over the faded lines. "These symbols - where did you get them?"

Eileen stepped forward, her voice steady despite the tension of the moment. "Scotland," she said. "We believe they're tied to Nazi interests in occult societies."

Beattie looked up, his gaze keen and almost amused. "Then you've certainly piqued my curiosity," he said. "Let's see if we can unravel this mystery together."

The team gathered around as Beattie began his analysis, his methodical approach bringing new clarity to their tangled web of intelligence. Eileen watched, feeling a cautious optimism take root amidst the uncertainty.

Beattie worked late into the night, his insights illuminating connections the team had only guessed at. Eileen stayed by his side, absorbing each revelation with growing determination. Accommodations had been set up at Bletchley for Eileen and the professor, so they decided to call it a night and resume the next day.

By late the next morning, they had mapped out a possible strategy that encompassed not just Albert's transmissions but the broader conspiracy that reached into unexpected corners of power and influence.

"I understand why the Nazis are interested in this. I possess a similar diagram and writings that allude to an ancient weapon.

This device, once considered a fantasy or legend by the ancients, was forgotten over time. It was discreetly distributed among a group within the Rosicrucian Order, who were possibly intrigued by science. Their scientific pursuits were frequently interwoven with their mystical beliefs and practices. Nevertheless, they broke away from the original order in the late 1700s," Professor Beattie concluded.

Beattie's revelation cast a long shadow over the morning at Bletchley Park. An ancient weapon, hidden through generations - now sought by factions unimaginable even in this world of spies and secrets. Eileen worked late, considering Beattie's findings with the team as they formulated how best to integrate them into their strategy. Arthur's leadership and constant focus were unyielding amidst the growing complexity of their mission.

"We'll need to tread carefully," he said to Eileen as they reviewed the latest intelligence reports. "If this information gets into the wrong hands..."

He didn't finish, but Eileen nodded. She understood the catastrophic potential all too well.

"What do you need from me?" she asked, ready to plunge deeper into the murky waters they'd found themselves in.

Arthur paused to think. "Professor, do you have any ideas on the best way to tackle this?"

"The first step," the professor replied, "is for me to go back to the university, examine the other diagram, and consult with some of my colleagues."

"Professor, could I speak to you in my office for a moment?" Arthur asked.

"Certainly," Beattie replied.

Eileen watched them leave, her mind racing with the implications of Beattie's knowledge. She returned to her desk, more determined than ever to uncover the extent of Albert's involvement and how deeply it connected to everything they were now untangling. The realization that her family played a crucial - if unwilling - part in this conspiracy lingered heavily.

The phone rang at dusk, its shrill insistence breaking her concentration. She answered to hear Arthur's voice, unexpectedly tense. "Eileen, I need you to meet us at once."

She barely took time to grab her coat as she left, the chill of the night air biting against her skin as she hurried through Bletchley's maze of buildings. Her heart pounded with anticipation and a flicker of dread.

Upon arriving at the specified office, she found Arthur along with Beattie and the senior officer. "The professor has completed the necessary paperwork and taken the oath, but for his protection, you and John will escort him back to the university."

Eileen's mind whirled with the unexpected turn. "You think he's in danger?" she asked, realizing as she spoke that the answer was obvious.

"Given what he knows, he's a target," Arthur replied. "We can't risk losing him - or the knowledge he carries."

Beattie consented with a wry smile. "Quite an adventure you've got me into," he said, his tone amused despite the gravity.

"Are you ready for this?" Arthur asked Eileen, his gaze searching hers for any sign of hesitation.

"I'm ready," she affirmed, the resolve in her voice mirrored by an inner steel. The stakes felt higher than ever, but so did her determination to see it through.

The plan moved quickly into action. John was summoned and briefed, his expression growing more serious with each detail.

"If we leave immediately, there's a night train," he said once they were alone.

They departed into the darkness, slipping out of Bletchley Park with Beattie in tow. Eileen felt the weight of their mission press heavily, each mile they travelled, a calculated risk. The first-class carriage was sparsely populated at this late hour, but Eileen remained vigilant, her eyes scanning for any sign of danger.

Beattie sat across from them, seemingly unfazed by the tension that thrummed beneath their journey. "You've got quite a knack for intrigue," he commented lightly, glancing between Eileen and John.

"We've had some practice," John replied, his tone more serious.

"But this is new ground for all of us." Eileen nodded, her thoughts racing through the possibilities. "How certain are you about the weapon?" she asked Beattie, needing to understand the stakes from his perspective.

He considered for a moment. "As certain as one can be with legends," he said. "But if the Nazis believe in its potential, that alone makes it dangerous."

They leaned back in their seats and dozed through the hours, each thinking of the possibilities ahead.

A car was waiting at the station to drive them to the university, its ancient buildings standing like sentinels against the encroaching threat. Beattie led them to his office, a book-lined sanctuary where the outside world seemed momentarily held at bay.

"We'll be safe here," he assured them.

Nonetheless, John checked out the halls, securing the area, his movements efficient and precise. Eileen felt a sense of calm in his presence, even as the weight of their mission pressed heavily upon them.

Beattie retrieved a worn box from his shelves, setting it on the desk with care. "This is what I mentioned," he said, unrolling another diagram, similar to the one they'd found in Scotland. His eyes were bright with the thrill of discovery. "But there are differences, notes and markings that suggest even greater possibilities."

Eileen studied the parchment, her breath catching at the intricacy of its design. "And you think these are instructions?" she asked, feeling both awed and apprehensive.

"Potentially," Beattie replied. "But they're encoded in ways we haven't yet deciphered."

Eileen's mind raced ahead, considering how this new piece fit into the puzzle they were assembling. "We'll need to get this back to Bletchley," she said decisively. "It's too critical to leave here."

John nodded in agreement, though his expression remained cautious.

Beattie watched them both with an air of calm confidence. "You two are remarkably well-suited for this work," he commented, a hint of admiration in his tone.

Eileen managed a tight smile. "Desperation makes for quick learners," she replied, though her mind was already plotting their next move.

John checked the train schedules and excused himself. When he returned, he had procured tickets for the afternoon train south.

Beattie suggested they go to the faculty dining room. While waiting to be served, one of the faculty members approached them and asked, "Is this what you were looking for last year? I just found it yesterday and remembered you mentioning it."

Beattie looked up, his surprise quickly changing to interest. "Ah, McAllister," he said, taking the book with a nod of gratitude. "Your timing is impeccable."

Eileen watched as Beattie thumbed through the pages, his expression one of deep concentration. Her pulse quickened. Could this be another key?

McAllister lingered, his curiosity evident. "Seems you've stirred up quite a fuss," he remarked, eyeing Eileen and John.

"We like to keep things interesting," John replied smoothly, his eyes on Beattie.

McAllister chuckled but seemed satisfied with not knowing more.

"I'll leave you to it, then," he said, retreating with a casual wave.

The moment he was out of earshot, Eileen leaned in. "What is it?"

Beattie set the book down on the table, his voice low but charged with excitement. "I nearly forgot about this volume," he said. "It's an older text; some consider it the Rosetta Stone of occult symbols. With this and the diagrams, we may have a chance at translating everything."

Hope surged in Eileen, a bright counterpoint to the shadow of doubt that had followed her for weeks. "Then we need to move fast," she said. "If Albert and the Nazis catch wind..."

Beattie nodded gravely. "Let's not give them the chance."

They finished their late breakfast quickly, the urgency of their discovery propelling them forward. Beattie gathered his critical documents, each one a thread that could unravel the complex web woven by history and ambition.

They returned, and Beattie secured his office and safely packed the diagrams. Eileen and John kept a close watch as they made their way to the waiting car. At the station, they boarded the train with an air of quiet determination. Eileen settled into her seat, clutching the precious documents tightly as the train pulled away from the platform. The miles stretched out like a taut string, each one drawing them closer to Bletchley and the enormity of what they now knew.

Beattie studied the landscape with a thoughtful expression. "You've both proven quite resourceful," he said, breaking the silence. "I'm glad to be in such capable hands."

Eileen exchanged a glance with John, feeling the weight of Beattie's words settle on her shoulders. It was an acknowledgment of their role but also a reminder of all that hung in the balance.

"We're just getting started," she replied, her resolve as firm as ever.

The journey back was tense but uneventful. They slept or read to pass the hours. Eileen's thoughts cycled through everything they'd uncovered—the ancient weapon, Albert's betrayals, and the possibility that hidden forces might yet turn the tide of war.

9

Ghosts of the Past

I t was dark when they arrived at Bletchley, and they felt as though they were stealing into the compound with heightened caution. Arthur met them.

"Any trouble?" he asked, his eyes scanning for signs of pursuit.

"Smooth enough," John replied, though the tension in his voice hinted at the weight of their discoveries.

Beattie looked invigorated by the journey. "The real work begins now," he said, a spark of intellectual excitement in his eyes.

Arthur led them to a secure briefing room where Eileen and John relayed everything they'd learned. Beattie laid out the diagrams and texts.

"This text," he said, gesturing to the book McAllister had provided, "may hold the key to translating Rosicrucian symbols and instructions. If we can decipher it fully, we'll not only understand what they're after but also how close they are to achieving it."

Eileen watched as the members of the team absorbed the implications, their expressions shifting from disbelief to grim determination.

"Go and get a good night's sleep. We'll get to work in the morning," Arthur said.

Early the next day, the analysts dove into their tasks, Beattie guiding them through the esoteric knowledge hidden for centuries. Eileen felt the weight of history pressing in on them, yet beneath it was an exhilaration she couldn't deny.

As the hours stretched into days, the full scope of their mission came into focus. The diagrams revealed secrets long buried, and with each new understanding, the stakes grew higher. Eileen scarcely noticed the exhaustion that tugged at her. Arthur's strategic mind wove together the disparate threads of information. He pulled Eileen aside more than once, his confidence in her abilities and instincts clear.

After days of intense work, they finally began to understand that they were looking at objects, as well as history. However, their breakthrough was suddenly interrupted by another urgent communication from London. News had arrived that Albert was on the move once more, spotted this time in Rosslyn near the ancient ruins. He was observed meticulously searching for clues, his gaze scanning the landscape with an intensity that suggested he was close to uncovering something significant.

Finlay contacted John to inform him that he had overheard a conversation in the cozy local pub involving someone he recognized, who matched Albert's description. He also mentioned that he might have found the location of another partial diagram.

John instructed Finlay to try to find more information.

As April warmed the grounds and primroses bloomed, tension hung over Bletchley like low-lying fog. Eileen worked tirelessly alongside Beattie and the team, each breakthrough in deciphering the diagrams bringing a fresh wave of urgency. The revelation of the ancient weapon - once dismissed as legend - loomed large, and the pieces began to align in ways that both thrilled and terrified.

Arthur drove the operation forward with relentless precision. He pulled Eileen aside one evening, his expression a mix of concern and determination.

"Albert's trail has gone cold again," he said. "We need you back in London. Your being there might help us flush him out."

Eileen nodded, feeling the familiar pull of duty even as her exhaustion threatened to overwhelm her. "I'll leave first thing," she replied.

The return to London was swift and uneventful. Each mile carried her further from the safety of Bletchley and deeper into the web of deception and betrayal that now defined her world.

Eileen arrived at her flat to find her sister-in-law in the midst of preparing their noon meal.

"Back again?" Francis asked, her tone teasing but with an edge of genuine surprise.

Eileen managed a weary smile. "Seems they can't do without me."

Francis set a steaming dish of stew in front of Eileen, watching her with a knowing look.

"You're going to wear yourself out, Eileen."

"I'm fine," she insisted, though the strain in her voice betrayed her fatigue. Francis poured her a cup of tea, her expression softening. "We worry, you know."

Eileen took the tea gratefully. The warmth seeped into her hands as she tried to relax amidst the familiar comforts of home.

"That's why I don't tell you too much," she joked gently, aware of how much she couldn't say.

They ate together, the easy rhythm of family life soothing even as Eileen's thoughts remained miles away. She slept fitfully that night. The next morning, she returned to Whitehall with a renewed sense of purpose, ready to dive back into the intrigue that awaited.

The office was a blur of activity. Reports piled high on Eileen's desk, and coded messages needed verification and analysis. She set to work with a single-minded focus, losing herself in the familiar rhythm of numbers and letters. But beneath the surface, she was attuned to every shift and whisper. She sensed Albert's presence like a shadow, his influence weaving through channels both seen and unseen. The possibility that he was using Bletchley's intelligence against them gnawed at her, driving her to redouble her efforts.

Word from Scotland came sporadically. Finlay was able to gain some valuable information from the locals and was feeding back critical insights, but there was no confirmation yet of Albert's exact location. Eileen read each message with a mix of hope and dread, knowing how close they were yet how easily it could all unravel.

A few days slipped by. Eileen moved through her tasks with a quiet determination, her life a cycle of train rides and tense anticipation. The pressure never relented, but she found strength in the knowledge that every decoded message, every obscured detail brought them closer to the truth. World War II cast a long shadow over London, its weight pressing down on the city and its inhabitants. The city bore the scars of the Blitz, and its streets were a testament to the resilience of its people. The sounds of the air raid sirens and the drone of enemy planes were ever-present in the memories of Londoners.

As spring gave way to summer, the war dragged on, and the people of London endured hardships and losses. Rationing and shortages had become a way of life. The city's spirit, however, like the flowers blooming in the ruins, remained unbroken. Despite the darkness, there were moments of unity and courage. People found solace in each other, forming unbreakable bonds.

Eileen navigated the treacherous paths of espionage with unwavering dedication, her talents recognized and valued by those around her. Then came a breakthrough, a message from Lieutenant Coleman, cryptic but clear: "New lead. Urgent developments." Eileen felt a thrill of exhilaration and risk as she read it.

Back at Bletchley, Arthur met her with an intensity that mirrored her own. "We've got movement on all fronts," he said. "Beattie's insights are shifting the entire operation."

Eileen absorbed the implications and threw herself back into work alongside Beattie and John, their combined efforts illuminating paths they hadn't dared hope for before.

"Albert's on the move again," Arthur reported one morning. "It's possible he's making a play for something big."

Eileen felt her pulse quicken. "And the diagram?"

"We think it's connected," Arthur replied.

The decision was made swiftly: Eileen would return to Scotland, this time with the full weight of their knowledge behind her. The risk was immense, but so were the potential rewards. She left Bletchley with John at her side, each step forward echoing with the stakes they now understood all too well. They arrived in Rosslyn late in the day, slipping into familiar territory.

Angus met them at the inn, his expression more serious than Eileen remembered. "I understand you require a missing piece for the diagram," he said abruptly.

"Yes," John responded.

"Okay, tomorrow morning, I'll show you where I believe we'll find the missing part of the diagram. It's been right under our noses all along. Try to get some rest; morning will arrive sooner than you expect," Angus remarked eagerly.

As the sun rose above the horizon, Eileen and John went down to breakfast in the dining room. Angus and Finlay arrived a few minutes later and sat down.

"Good morning, did ye have a good sleep?" Angus remarked

"Not really," said John, "too excited."

"Let's get some breakfast," he suggested.

The owner approached, and Angus made the introductions, stating, "Meet Hamish McTague, the fifth generation to manage this esteemed establishment."

"So, Angus tells me you're looking for the Rosicrucian diagram that could be a clue to your missing piece," he said, leaning over the table and speaking quietly.

He was exercising some caution because Angus and Finlay had informed him about the group that had assaulted him a few months earlier, and a few businessmen were reading the morning paper over their breakfast toast.

They had a short conversation, and Hamish took their order.

"Breakfast is on the house, enjoy!" Hamish quipped. Then he disappeared into the kitchen.

"Does he know what we are looking for?" said John.

"I can't tell you with these strangers in the room," Angus muttered, his voice low and cautious.

Eileen, sensing his discomfort, scanned the room. Her eyes caught on a solitary man seated four tables away. He was impeccably dressed in a tailored suit, his polished shoes gleaming under the soft light. A steaming cup of coffee rested in front of him, and he was engrossed in the local newspaper, its pages rustling gently with his movements.

"Yes," she whispered, barely audible over the hum of conversation. "I think I recognize that gentleman by the window. He's been on the train with us recently." The whisper carried a note of intrigue, as if the man's presence was a puzzle waiting to be solved.

Hamish came out during breakfast and said, "Is everything to your liking?" Everyone nodded in agreement.

John grabbed his arm and said in a low whisper, "Do you know that gentleman over by the window? "

"Oh, yes," Hamish said, "That's Thomas Richardson. He's a manager for Pye Radio. He looks after this area, so he says."

Finlay casually turned around and immediately halted. "That's the person who was observing us at the ruins the other day," he said.

"Are you certain?" Angus asked.

"Yes, I recognize the scar on his cheek," Finlay replied.

They finished breakfast, but the person they were curious about left before they could get a proper look at him. As everyone departed on their separate paths, Hamish emerged and said, "Come with me, and I'll show you what I believe is the missing puzzle piece."

They rose from their seats and trailed behind Hamish to the far side of the dining room, where there was an antique curio cabinet. The cabinet, with its intricate woodwork and the patina of age, appeared to be a cherished heirloom that had been passed down through the family for generations.

"When Angus mentioned that you were searching for clues related to a map or something similar, and I glanced at some of the symbols you found, it brought back a vivid memory. These symbols bore a striking resemblance to the intricate designs my great-grandfather meticulously carved when he crafted the cabinet."

As the cabinet door creaked open, Eileen peered inside, her eyes adjusting to the dim interior. As Hamish opened one of the doors, the light from the dining room windows revealed a series of cryptic symbols etched into the wood, their intricate patterns casting shadows along the surface. Eileen felt a shiver of excitement at the discovery.

"There you see. I told you it was under our noses," Angus replied.

At that moment, John observed a shadow of a person staring in the window. Finlay shot outside only to see the back of the person he thought he'd watched at the breakfast table.

He closed the drapes. "We need to get Beattie up here to look at this and conduct a proper investigation."

At that moment, Hamish said, "I don't want anyone arousing any suspicions with the guests."

"Then we move quickly," Eileen said, her resolve firm. "John will make the arrangements. Angus, can you and Finlay keep things quiet until we're back?"

"Aye," Angus agreed, his voice tinged with urgency. "But get a move on."

She and John sent an encrypted message to Bletchley, outlining the situation and requesting immediate support. The response was swift and decisive; Beattie would arrive within the day.

"We'll need to be ready when he gets here. It would be best if the cabinet were in some more private room," John said, his gaze steady on Eileen's.

"Let's talk to Hamish," she said, her mind already spinning through possibilities and plans.

That afternoon, a local mover arrived and began moving new kitchen cabinets into the inn's kitchen. This gave John an idea. He said he would like to move the cabinet to their lab to analyze it.

As he was talking to Hamish, the movers were setting things up, and Hamish said, "I'm not comfortable letting it leave with strangers. That's going to arouse a lot of curiosity with the locals."

John agreed. "What if we get your movers to build a crate and transport it back to Bletchley Park?"

Hamish and John went to the kitchen to talk to the mover. "Robert, this is John, and he has purchased my cabinet in the dining room, and he needs you to deliver it to this address." He handed him the address - Sherwood Dr, Bletchley, Milton Keynes.

"That's a bit farther than I'm willing to go," Robert explained.

"We'll cover all your expenses and find you the petrol," John assured them. Robert glanced at Hamish, who nodded and said, "I trust John."

"Well, that's good enough for me," Robert replied.

"Meanwhile, I'd like Professor Beattie to come here and take another similar piece to confuse Albert, if you agree, Hamish?

"Aye, I have just the piece."

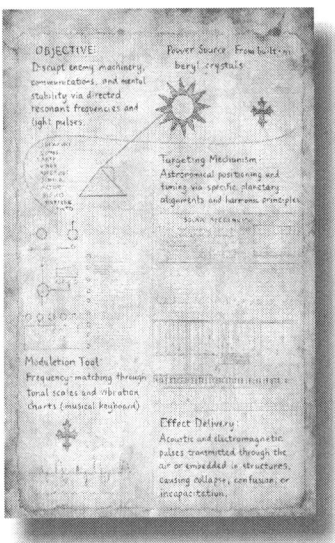

10

The Clues are Emerging

Eileen and John headed back by train to Bletchley. The cabinet arrived the following day, its ancient wood protected by a crate that bore the tell-tale marks of haste. Eileen watched as it was unloaded, her heart pounding with anticipation. She knew they needed to act swiftly; others would not be far behind.

Arthur met her as the crate was opened. "Is this what I think it is?" he asked, taking in the intricate symbols.

Eileen nodded, her fingers brushing lightly over the carved designs. "It's part of the diagram," she said. "And I think Albert knows we're onto it."

The team gathered quickly, their focus intense as they began examining every inch of the cabinet. They wished Beattie was with them, but for their deception to work he needed to spend time in Rosslyn.

"Let's take this to the lab and get to work on it immediately," Arthur instructed.

They moved with precision, transporting the cabinet to a secure room where they could document and analyze every detail of it. Eileen and the other analysts used their collective expertise to drive the operation forward with relentless focus. The hours stretched long into the night as they cataloged each symbol, each marking. Eileen felt a surge of exhilaration with every new discovery, knowing they were peeling back layers of secrecy that had remained hidden for generations.

After two days in Scotland, Beattie returned, anxious to see the clue they had spirited out of the inn. "Remarkable," he murmured when he laid eyes on it. These markings are unlike anything I've seen."

Eileen said, "I think there is more to it than meets the eye."

"This back panel," Beattie said, gesturing to a section with an unusual concentration of symbols. "I suspect it conceals something more."

They meticulously searched for a secret lock or mechanism that could open the back. They spotted two appliqués at the top of the back panel, but pressing or turning them had no effect. Then they discovered four wooden dowels beneath the cabinet.

Professor Beattie suggested, "These might be a clue because they are out of place. Let's lay it down." Observing that the dowels had been sealed with linseed oil, he requested a heat gun. After cautiously heating each dowel to soften the oil, he extracted them, revealing a thin wire attached to each. However, the wires remained immobile, leaving them perplexed, until someone suggested trying the appliqués again.

Turning each appliqué simultaneously in the opposite direction caused the dowels to shift downward, enabling them to move the outer panel and unveil an inner panel with a mysterious diagram and what appeared to be a schematic.

"This confirms it," he said, pointing to a set of markings that mirrored those on his own diagram. "The Rosicrucian connection is undeniable. I suggest we remove this and replace it with a fake to ensure it directs Albert onto a different path."

90

Eileen watched. "If we can translate this final piece," she said, "we'll know exactly what this diagram was meant to represent and why."

Arthur's expression was grim but determined. "And if we don't?"

Eileen felt the weight of his words. "We will," she replied, her voice steady.

The team worked around the clock, crafting a fake diagram that could be used to mislead anyone who might intercept it. The team remained focused and never wavered, each move calculated to keep them one step ahead of Albert and the growing threat he represented.

Within days, they had what they needed: a meticulously reproduced fake diagram that could withstand close scrutiny. The real diagram was secured, its secrets now within reach thanks to Beattie's insights and Eileen's relentless pursuit.

Arthur called a meeting as soon as the fake diagram was installed in the cabinet. "We have an opportunity here to deliver this back to the inn and see if someone is interested in it."

The movers, after their two-day holiday, loaded the cabinet back into the van and left on the journey to Scotland.

The next morning, the analysts began to work on the diagram. "Beattie's insights have given us a crucial edge," Arthur replied. "With these new translations, we can accelerate our operations and tighten our net around Albert's network. Their interest in the occult and ancient technology suggests they're pursuing multiple strategies simultaneously. This buys us some time but also indicates they may have other plans in motion."

The diagrams and book revealed a chilling depth to the Rosicrucians' ancient technologies and mystical beliefs that merged with their ambitions and beliefs. Were they planning on creating a weapon? Had they already created something that had yet to be deployed?

With each decoded message and translated symbol, they hoped they were gaining ground.They couldn't believe what they had discovered. The Rosicrucians seemed to be able to harness the earth's vibrational and sound frequencies to create a machine that could affect a human's ability to function.

A few days later. Arthur came into the hut... "I've just received a report from Hamish that someone entered the inn last night, broke open the back of the cabinet and took the fake diagram. This means we either have a mole in our organization or someone observed us the day you were looking at the cabinet."

Later that afternoon, Professor Beattie collected everyone together. "Before you is a preliminary report that we put together. Based on our findings so far, I believe, with your support, Lieutenant Coleman, that we need to find individuals who can help create a blueprint for a classified experimental weapon."

The weight of the project, a significant undertaking with far-reaching implications, settled upon them as they embarked on the new phase of their critical mission.

The days that followed were filled with anticipation and excitement as the new members of the team worked on the material at hand and considered how they could possibly harness this theoretical knowledge to their advantage.

By the end of July, Professor Beattie and the team were able to present a report to Arthur. We think this diagram appears to be a complex, almost mystical schematic blending scientific notation, astronomy, music, and esoteric geometry. Here's a speculative breakdown imagining it as an experimental weapon:

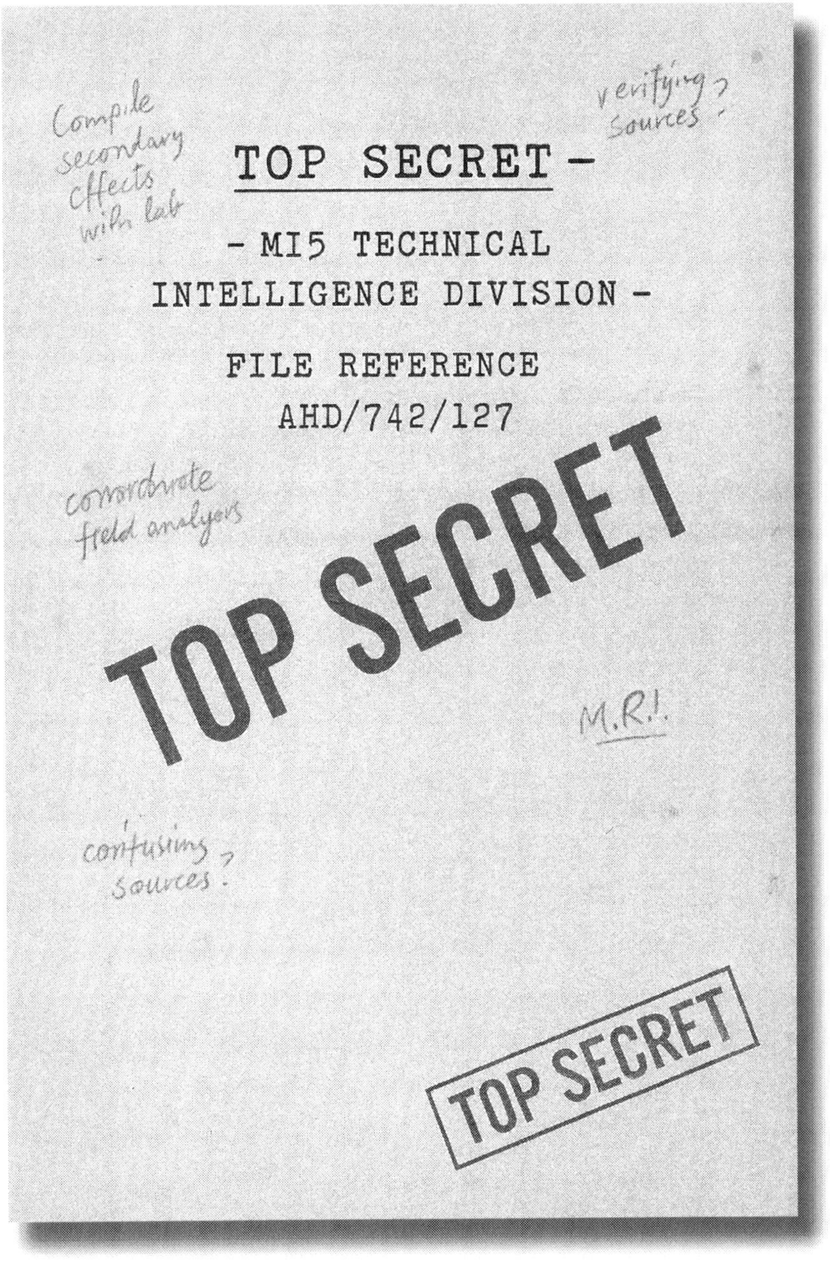

TOP SECRET —

- MI5 TECHNICAL
INTELLIGENCE DIVISION -

FILE REFERENCE
AHD/742/127

TOP SECRET

TOP SECRET

Compile secondary effects with lab

verifying? sources?

coordinate field analysis

M.R.I.

confusing? sources?

TOP SECRET

See
attached
sketch

TOP SECRET

– M15 TECHNICAL INTELLICENCE DIVISION –
FILE REFERENCE: AHD/742/127

Sun Diagram & Light Ray (Top Center)

- The sun at cop emists focused ray into triangular prism possibly simolight refraction or focused energy transmission:
- This triangle (a sacred Rosicrucian symbol) could represent "The Trinity of Forces: Sound, Light, and Vibration.
- This light beam might refer to solar-powered energy focusing, perhaps for long-range energy transfer or resonance generation.

Planetary Alignments & Moons (Upper Left)

- Lists planets and their moons, emphasizing gravitational and vibrational relationships. Rosicrucians believed celestial bodles emitted cosmic harmonies Monsmidane
- This part may tie into timing weapon use with astronomical alignments, exploiting gravitational fields to amplify effects— possibly influencing tides, EM fields, or seismic activity).

TOP SECRET

Keyboard & Frequencies (Bottom Right)

- A musical keyboard labeled with notes, letters, and frequency markings— This might be a frequency targeting system – matching musical tones with human brainwave points, or enemy infrastructure vulnerabilitys.
- Likely intended for resonance-based usruton (e.g., shattering materials, confusing communications, inducing nausea or cofusion in enemy troops).

Flowchart / Circuit-like Diagram (Lower Left)

- Might represent energy conversion or modulation steps— a primitive analog design for converting solar energy → electrical signals → modulated frequencies.
- This could simulate sound wave propagation, ideal for acoustic testing of structures or living targets, echoing early concepts of infrasound weapons.

Flowchart / Circuit-like Diagram (Lower Left)

- Might represent energy conversion or modulation steps— a primitive analogdesign for converting solar energy → electrical signals → modulated frequencies.

Objective: Disrupt enemy machinery, communications, and mental stability via directed resonant frequencies and light pulses.

- Power Source: Solar energy (symbolized by the sun.).
- Targeting Mechanism: Astronomagnet positioning and tuning via specific planetary alignments and harmonic principles.
- Modulation Tool: Frequency-matching through tonal scales and vibration charts (musical keyboard).
- Effect Delivery: Acoustic and electronagnetic pulses transmitted through the air or or embedded in structures, causing collapse, confusion, or incapacitation.

Rosicrucian Influence:
- The Rosicrucians believed that music, light, and sacred geometry could shape reality.
- Their rituals often involved vibrations and attunements designed to reach higher consciousness or influence environments.
- This chart may have encoded both scientific experimentation and spiritual philosophy making the weapon a blend of technological mysticism, very in line with wartime experimentation.

TOP SECRET

TOP SECRET

Conclusion:

This diagram could represent a cloaked metaphysical and music language to obscure its true purpose. Whether meant to manipulate structures, soldiers, or minds, it reflects an era when science, secrecy, and the occult intersected–and when ancient orders like the Rosicrucians may have inspired unconventional warfare strategies.

The team delved deeper into the intricacies of the Rosicrucian diagram, their curiosity piqued by the enigmatic symbols and their potential implications. The physicist in their group suggested another of the code breakers who held an advanced degree in Physics be brought to consider the possibility that such a weapon could be produced. Someone else said that one of the code breakers was an acoustics expert. Arthur, ever the astute leader, recognized the significance of their findings and the need for specialized expertise.

Both new team members were amazed.

"The Rosicrucians seem to have a profound understanding of wave interactions and their potential applications." The acoustics expert traced his finger along the intricate patterns, his mind considering possibilities. "With this knowledge, they could have theoretically created a device capable of harnessing and manipulating sound and light waves for various purposes."

Eileen, ever the intrepid agent, asked the question that was on everyone's minds. "Could they have built such a device? And if so, what would its capabilities be?"

The room fell silent. "It's difficult to say with certainty. But if I had to speculate, I'd say they were attempting to create a device that could generate powerful resonance waves. The question is, what was their intended target?"

The team exchanged glances, each of them knowing all too well the potential devastation such a device could unleash. John, his sharp mind already turning over the possibilities, spoke up. "If we assume their target was human, the implications are dire. A device like that could cause immense harm, even death."

"How would they have a power source of this magnitude in the 17th century or before?" asked Professor Beattie.

The team were unanimous in their belief that the ancients might have had sources of power and energy far more advanced than anyone in this era imagined. Intriguingly, their analyses revealed a strange, recurring motif within the schematics—a glyph echoing Rosicrucian symbology and eerily reminiscent of humanity's age-old quest: to tap into the planet's magnetic heart and exploit its resonant energies. They speculated on whether the Rosicrucians had indeed constructed a device in its most primitive form. Could they have harnessed this power centuries before it was thought of in the twentieth century? The idea was both thrilling and terrifying, suggesting that their knowledge ran deeper than anyone had dared to believe.

If the Nazis believed they could replicate these discoveries, they would stop at nothing to obtain them. Each new revelation brought with it an urgency that drove the team to work around the clock.

11

A Race Against Time

Another telegram arrived from Scotland, this time more straightforward: "Found another site," Finlay had written. "Need you soonest."

Eileen felt a familiar thrill of risk and opportunity as she read it. "We need to go again," she said. Arthur agreed. "We'll send you with the two new members of the team," he said. "We can't leave anything to chance."

Eileen prepared to return north, the stakes higher than ever. She and John boarded the train with a sense of déjà vu.

They arrived at the inn, finding Angus and Finlay waiting in the bar with grim expressions. Angus greeted them, his weathered face creased with concern. "We're glad ye could come," he said, his Scottish brogue thick and his eyes narrowing as he surveyed the group. "It's not often we come across a site like this. Finlay and I accidentally stumbled upon it, but we know it's important.".

"Can you take us to the site tomorrow?" John asked.

"Aye," Angus agreed.

The following morning, Eileen and John, with Harry and James, who would provide fresh observations and were eager to see where the mysterious diagrams originated, assembled after an early breakfast in the Inn's dining room.

"Lead the way," Eileen said, waving them ahead of her. As they ventured further from town, the landscape grew increasingly wild and rugged. Angus navigated the twisting roads with ease, his old van bouncing along the potholed tracks. The team exchanged nervous glances; the weight of their mission lay heavily on their minds. Finally, they reached a secluded glen, the site nestled amidst ancient trees and rolling hills. The air was warm with the scent of summer and the noise of insects.

"This way," Angus pointed, his voice hushed as if respecting the secrets the place held. The group followed, their footsteps crunching on the gravel path. Eileen's heart raced as she anticipated what they might uncover. Angus slowed, his gaze flicking to the surrounding forest as if expecting something to leap out at them. Then, he stopped abruptly, his face illuminated by the morning light filtering through crooked hawthorne trees.

"Here we are," he announced, his voice echoing in the quiet glen. Eileen drew a sharp breath as she beheld the scene before them.

A broken ring of granite, each boulder impossibly precise, choked the breath from Eileen. The central platform, a monolith of chilling grey, loomed like a tombstone. "What is this place?" she breathed.

Finlay, his youthful face etched with a grim fascination, shook his head. His blue eyes, usually sparkling with mischief, were shadowed.

"We don't know for certain, Ma'am. Angus here…" he gestured to the man beside him.

"I think it's an ancient… gathering place, I suspect," Angus rumbled, his voice a gravelly whisper that seemed to echo from the stones themselves. "Aye, there be many such scattered across the isles… more than most realize." His words hung heavy, laced with a cryptic warning.

John surveyed the scene, his gaze sharp and appraising, before speaking in a low, controlled tone. "Let's document this. Photographs, detailed sketches, measurements. Every detail." As they circled the structure, the scent of damp earth and decaying vegetation heavy in the air, Eileen stumbled. She pointed a trembling finger at a series of deeply etched symbols carved into one of the stones.

"John... look! These... these are identical to the Rosicrucian diagrams!"

A low growl rumbled from John's chest.

"Harry."

The young acoustics specialist stood rigid. "Yes, sir."

"Use the metal detector; you never know what lies beneath."

Harry began a methodical search of the area, and the inner circle, covered with sand, started to create strange circular patterns. Both the sand and the patterns were unusual. Harry signalled everyone over to look at the phenomenon.

The physicist, James, said he had studied the Chladni effect in physics at university.

John immediately responded with, "What is the Chladni effect?"

"Well, Sir, it's caused by vibrational resonance. When it's set to a certain frequency, the vibration causes the sand to move and concentrate, which can form geometric shapes. The patterns formed by these lines are now known as Chladni figures. Similar nodal patterns can also be found by assembling micro-scale materials on Faraday waves."

John was stunned by this discovery. "How is this anomaly actually working?"

Harry explained, "I think it's the metal detector, which operates at between 3-100 kHz, utilizing two coils: one as a transmitter that emits the electromagnetic field and another as a receiver that detects any signals reflected from metal objects. I think we have some metal buried under here."

John gave the order to excavate the area. As Harry and James began to excavate, the tension grew. What could possibly be happening to cause these strange effects? They knew that whatever lay buried here was connected to the mysterious activities and the potential involvement with the Rosicrucians.

"Sir, we've hit some kind of metal object," Harry said, his brow furrowed in concentration as he brushed away the dirt. He was very warm in the July heat and wiped his forehead as he stood leaning on the shovel.

"Keep digging," John ordered, his gaze fixed on the object. "Eileen, take a look at this." The metal object was unlike anything they had seen so far. It seemed to be approximately three feet in diameter, and as they dug deeper, it was well anchored below the surface. Etched into the structure were cryptic Rosicrucian markings. Harry and the team were still digging, and they had managed to clear away enough dirt to reveal the symbols. John got out a camera and started to take photos. As they continued their excavation, a sense of awe hung heavy in the air. Eileen, John, and the others watched with bated breath as Harry and his James carefully brushed away the dirt, revealing more of the enigmatic metal object.

Angus stood to the side, his weathered face a mask. As the symbols were slowly uncovered, a spark of recognition flashed in his eyes. He had seen those markings before, in a book he had acquired many years ago. It was an ancient tome, its pages filled with mysterious diagrams and arcane knowledge. Angus had always suspected that the book held a connection to forbidden practices and secret societies, but he had never imagined encountering physical evidence of its existence. The symbols seemed to dance before his eyes, stirring long-forgotten memories. Angus's heart raced as he realized the significance of this discovery.

104

Angus grabbed John's arm and said, "Those symbols, laddie... I've encountered them before. They're in an old book at the Rosslyn Chapel." John looked at Angus and decided to stop the dig and get the photos developed. Let's call it a day and head back into town. Based on what we have uncovered, we will have to station a security detail here for the night.

As the sun descended, casting long shadows across the ancient site, the group returned along the winding road to Rosslyn, their minds racing with questions and a mounting sense of urgency. They needed to find a local photographer to develop their pictures of the metal object and the cryptic markings.

Angus knew an amateur photographer who lived and worked in Rosslyn. In the fading light, they found his quaint photography studio. The photographer, a bespectacled man with silver hair, welcomed them in and listened intently as they explained their predicament. With a nod of understanding, he promised to develop the photos as quickly as possible, his eyes sparkling with curiosity.

The next morning, armed with the developed photographs, the five of them set out for Rosslyn Chapel. The abbey loomed before them, its ancient stones weathered by time. They were greeted by the caretaker, Bruce Andrews, a stooped figure with a wise, weathered face. His eyes widened as he recognized Angus.

"Angus, old friend, what brings you here this damp morning and who are your companions?"

"These people are from London and they work for MI5," Angus explained.

Bruce looked at them with curiosity and said, "I've heard about all the commotion in town and at the ruins, so I was wondering how long it might take you to find your way here. There was a fellow here a couple of days ago, and he spent a long time poking around at the Chapel."

"How so?" said John.

"Well, he looked through the graveyard and at the carvings on the inside walls. Then he was asking me if I knew about the ancient symbols and if they were connected to the Rosicrucians."

"What did you tell him?" Eileen said with a stern look.

"Well, based on the rumours in town and the fact that he was alone and didn't have a good feeling about him or his question, I sent him on his way. Around these parts, you should have a local like Angus or Finlay to accompany you."

That's a relief, Eileen thought.

"Well, Bruce, you can trust these folks," said Angus with a friendly smile. "We have some photos that we think you would be very interested in."

"Well, come in and we'll have a look," Bruce said with anticipation.

The man guided them through a small side entrance into the dark crypt. As they descended, he reached out for a lamp and switched it on, filling the space with a warm glow. The soft light provided a sense of comfort, a welcome contrast to the eerie atmosphere of the underground.

The cool stone walls and musty air of the basement surrounded them, but the glow of the lamp reassured them. The gentle illumination revealed the way forward, guiding them deeper into the depths of the Chapel. They followed the man, their hands brushing against the rough walls, until they reached their destination. Bruce opened a locked door to his workshop and they laid the photos out on his workbench. Bruce looked intensely at them for a few minutes.

"Some of these symbols appear on the Abbey walls and ceiling upstairs," he said. "There has been many a person over the years with all kinds of theories about the symbols and their possible meanings, everything from the Knights Templar to Alien visitations. Come over here," he said, pointing to the side of the room. "I have something that may shed some light on this."

There, in a dusty corner, was a cabinet fastened to the wall. He opened the door with an old skeleton key, revealing some gardening tools and spare parts for the old boiler. He removed everything and pushed in a knot in the wood, which opened a hidden wooden door, revealing an old wall safe with a combination lock that used letters to unlock it.

"Look away while I dial the combination," Bruce said.

Years of neglect were evident as the door groaned open, its hinges protesting with a rusty sigh. Inside lay a device unlike anything they had ever seen. Bruce carefully picked up the device, a 6" rod with six small discs and ten symbols around each one, and a blank disc in the middle with another six discs with ten symbols, and gears at one end.

Bruce showed the device to everyone.

John took a look at it and commented, "Anyone guess what this would be used for?"

Angus, his eyes gleaming, shook his head slowly. "I've seen my fair share of old artifacts, but this... this is something else entirely."

Finlay, his youthful face alight with excitement, asked, "Do you think it could be a mechanism to unlock the secrets of this place?"

Bruce said, "Legend has it that the device was placed here by Robert Wentworth Little, a Rosicrucian in the 1850s and was shrouded in mystery as to what it was used for. I found the safe by accident years ago, and we had no idea how to open it until one of the parishioners' relatives, a locksmith, came down from Edinburgh and figured out the code based on some of the stone carvings in the chapel."

"May we examine the device back at our lab?" asked John.

"Yes, if you promise to bring it back in one piece," said Bruce.

"Of course, you have my word."

Bruce led the way, ushering them up to the chaplain's office. With a grand gesture, he pulled a large book from a shelf. He opened it, revealing a cutout section with a small notebook inside. "This book will help you figure out the device's possible use," he said.

John asked Bruce if they could go on a quick tour of the Chapel. Bruce's eyes lit up.

The sun shone through the stained glass windows, casting vibrant colours across the ancient stone walls. The carvings seemed to come to life in the light, their intricate details and delicate curves catching the eye.

Bruce led the way, pointing out each carving with a childlike wonder. The tour was quiet, save for the occasional gasp or whisper of awe. The Abbey was a masterpiece, and in the stillness, every detail could be appreciated. It was a serene experience, one that left a lasting impression on all who were lucky enough to witness it.

Angus noticed something amiss as the team left the Chapel. A figure, partially hidden in the shadows of the surrounding gravestones, was observing them.

He signalled to John. John, his senses equally attuned, moved to position himself protectively in front of the group.

"Who's out there?" John's voice cut through the silence.

The figure stepped forward. The stranger was tall and thin, but well-groomed.

Eileen's curiosity battled with her instinctive wariness as she took a cautious step forward, her eyes never leaving the mysterious figure. "Who are you, and what are you doing here?" she demanded, her voice steady despite the questions racing through her mind.

"I've been expecting you and your people," the stranger said, "I know why you're here, and I can help you." Eileen's mind raced. Could this stranger be an ally or another piece in Albert's treacherous game? She exchanged a glance with John, their unspoken communication conveying a shared sense of caution.

"What do you know?" John asked, his voice firm.

The stranger's smile widened, and he took a step forward, his eyes flicking to the ancient structure of the Abbey and then back to the group.

The young physicist made a startled noise. "I recall seeing you at the university."

"My name is Thomas Richardson, and I am, as the young man says, a professor at the University of Edinburgh. I know the secrets of the book and device you hold," he whispered. "And I know the danger you're facing, and I can offer you knowledge, and perhaps, a way to stop the Nazis."

The team weighed their options. The promise of answers and the prospect of a powerful ally were enticing, but could they trust this person?

Eileen's determination shone in her eyes, and she took a step forward. "We're listening," she said, her voice steady.

"What I'm about to reveal will change everything you have become accustomed to in your thinking, your understanding of science, and even your understanding of history. The book describes a long, cylinder-like mechanism similar to what you have just discovered. It has 12 discs, 10 symbols, and a blank disc in the middle."

"You said you were expecting us?" John questioned.

"Yes, I have been teaching history and ancient archeology, and I overheard John and Eileen one night in the library talking with Professor Beattie. I had to act; so, I started to follow the trail, and it led to the Inn. I was in the dining room at the time and waited until you finished and left. Then I watched through the window and observed enough to learn you were on the right path. I have been looking for the diagram that you stumbled upon. It's a secret weapon developed by the ancients. Now that we have this device, we may be able to activate it. According to my father's notes, there were plans to build it, and a working model may exist."

Angus, his weathered face alight with curiosity, spoke up. "So, what now? We have a device, but what is this secret weapon?"

John quickly changed the conversation, knowing that Bruce and Angus were becoming privy to more information than they needed to know. "Well, everyone, let's call it a day, head back to the Inn."

"Thank you, Professor. Would you be available to meet us next week at Bletchley Park to help decipher this device?"

"Yes, indeed, I can pack and meet you at the Inn in the morning."

"Good. We will leave on the first train," John responded. Later that day, John urgently contacted Bletchley Park via telegraph to check Professor Richardson's credentials.

12

The Mysterious Stranger

The next morning, the sun bathed the dining room of Hamish's inn in a warm glow. Eileen, John and Professor Richardson gathered for breakfast. John had received confirmation that Professor Richardson was, indeed, part of the faculty at the university. The atmosphere was electric with anticipation as they eagerly awaited the day's adventures. They carefully avoided any discussion of their recent discoveries, opting instead for light-hearted banter.

As they indulged in their breakfast, Hamish, the jovial host, approached their table, his curiosity piqued by their air of secrecy. "Good morning, friends," he greeted them. "I can sense the excitement in the air. Any new developments on your project?"

John, with a mischievous smile, replied, "All I can say, Hamish, is that we have some very positive news. But, unfortunately, I'm not at liberty to divulge the details just yet."

Hamish feigned disappointment, but his interest was piqued. "I understand completely," he said, his tone conveying a hint of playful frustration. "Well, when you're ready to share, I'll be all ears."

At that moment, Eileen seized the opportunity to introduce Professor Richardson more formally. "Hamish, allow me to introduce Professor Thomas Richardson from Edinburgh University. He's joining us on this fascinating journey."

Hamish, taken aback, exclaimed, "A professor, are you? I must admit, I thought you were a salesperson with your dashing briefcase. My apologies for the mistake."

Professor Richardson, with a twinkle in his eye, gracefully accepted the apology. "No need to apologize, Hamish. I understand the confusion. The label on my briefcase was intended to do that, and I must say, the disguise allowed me to get closer to the project unnoticed."

As they concluded their breakfast, the trio bid Hamish farewell and made their way to the train station, eager to return to Bletchley Park. The journey back was filled with lively conversation and speculation about their ongoing investigation. Eileen asked the professor about his expertise and how it tied into their mission. Professor Richardson, always eager to impart knowledge, shared fascinating insights into his academic pursuits and how they intersected with their current endeavour.

The next afternoon, back at Bletchley, they had a meeting with Arthur and Professor Beattie. Professor Beattie greeted Richardson warmly.

"How have you been, man? I have to say I wasn't expecting you to play a part in this."

"Well, James, I overheard a conversation you were having with Eileen and John that day at the university, and it piqued my curiosity. You see, I have been studying my great-great-grandfather's history and his lifelong interest in the Rosicrucian Order."

John piped in, "Yes, Richardson was there the day we discovered the secret document that was hidden in the cabinet at the inn. He was the one looking in the window, not Albert, as we had originally assumed."

"Well, what discoveries have you unearthed?"

"It turns out a key that was part of this mystery went missing years ago. The stone circle edifice at the ruins site was a regular meeting place of the local Rosicrucian order. I knew that you might be back, so I had the local train station attendant, who is a friend of mine, keep an eye out for you. That day, I waited out of sight, hoping you would find the missing key with your metal detector."

"We have to be cautious," John began, his deep voice filling the room. "With Professor Richardson now in the mix, our actions will be under even greater scrutiny. We need to plan our next steps carefully."

Eileen admired John's calm demeanour, and his naval intelligence officer training served him well in these moments of heightened tension.

Arthur suggested they continue with their normal activities for a while as the newer members of the team research the device and its connection to the order. "I'll get hold of a mechanical engineer and a locksmith to study this new device," Arthur said.

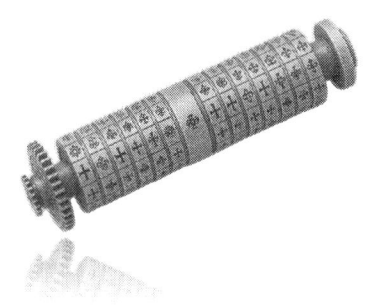

13

The Key to the Mystery

Eileen volunteered to work with them as they studied the device and felt a buzz of anticipation as they settled into Hut 7. Eileen concentrated on the patterns of the intricate designs, each one unique yet somehow interconnected.

A week had passed, and Major Williams, who was in charge of the engineering division at Bletchley, came in to review their progress. "Any clues, people?"

Arthur stood up and introduced the Major to everyone.

Robert, one of the mechanical engineers, said, "We've made some progress, but we're having a hard time trying to figure out how it functions."

Leonard, the locksmith, who had been brought in from London and had over 40 years of experience working for the royal family and their vast properties, was also puzzled about how it worked. Then all of a sudden he said, "I've got it, see these symbols," pointing to the forging in the handle.

"Yes," said Williams, "go on."

"They need to be aligned in a certain sequence. I've seen something similar in the Tower of London crown jewels vault." Lenard continued, "It has two parts: the first set of 6 rings has internal magnets that, when lined up on the outside of the lock, will activate the second set of rings inside the lock, which will in turn allow you to open the internal mechanism." He paused and then, looking at some point on the ceiling as he did the calculations, said,

"The total number of possible combinations for the cipher lock, we need to know:

Number of rings: 12
Number of symbols per ring: Let's assume each ring has 10 unique Rosicrucian symbols (based
on what is visible on the discs, with multiple symbol variants like crosses, flowers, stars, etc.)
Formula:
Total combinations = (symbols per ring) number of rings = 10/12th
1,000,000,000,000 (1 trillion combinations)."

Professor Richardson interrupted Leonard. "According to my great-grandfather's notes, each key is created to open each device; they are made together, and unlike today's tumbler locks, which can be rekeyed, this can't."

Just then, one of the staff came in and pulled John and Major Williams aside, whispering.

"We have a problem, sir. Finlay has reported that people have been seen poking around the Chapel and asking questions at the ruins.

"Carry on here, all of you. John, Eileen, follow me," Williams said.

"Your man, Finlay and the farmer Callum have observed your Schulte snooping around the Chapel and the ruins. We need you to make a trip up there and try to find out what's going on.

"What about the key, Sir?" John said, questioning the next move.

Williams replied, "Coleman, you take care of this end."

With that, John and Eileen made arrangements to catch the next available train, and this time Finlay met them at the station. "Good evening, Finlay."

"Good evening, sir, ma'am. I hope you had a nice journey." As they walked to his car, they were both excited and apprehensive about Albert and the so-called Nazi sympathizers.

"What have you been observing, Finlay?" Eileen said.

"Well, ma'am, A few days ago, the man you call Albert was asking Hamish some questions about the inn and its history, and Albert said he was curious because his parents had a similar establishment in London, but when Hamish confronted him about the location and name of the Inn in London, Albert quickly turned and said he had to go. Bruce and I have been keeping a close eye on the Chapel, and we noticed evidence of the digging and the gravestones overturned. That's when Bruce alerted the Police, and they arrested Albert."

"What?"

"Yes, sir," said Finlay. "He is in custody."

"Why was he arrested?"

"Well, sir, that's an historical site, and if you disturb the gravestones or the structure, you are in violation of the local heritage laws."

John immediately said, "Take us to the police station."

"Yes, sir."

When they arrived, John and Eileen entered the building, and John told Finlay to remain with the car. They approached the front desk.

"Yes, sir. Can I help you?"

"We understand you arrested a gentleman in connection with the ruins just outside of town."

"Yes, sir. He is awaiting a court appearance tomorrow," said the constable.

"That won't be necessary. We'll take over from here." He held up his MI5 ID.

"Just a minute, please." Then the constable called out. "Sir, can you come out here?"

"What's the problem, Constable?"

"These people are from the Secret Service, and they want to take the gentleman we arrested yesterday into custody."

The sergeant, looking very curious, said, "Come into my office. Have a seat. Can I get either of you a cup of tea?"

"Yes, said Eileen. "I would love one."

"And you, sir?"

"No, thank you," said John.

"Ian."

"Yes, sir."

"Tea and what passes as biscuits these days, if there are any left, please."

"Yes, Sergeant."

The courtesies taken care of, Eileen and John explained the situation, filling the local officer in on some details of their operation and Albert's potential threat.

The sergeant, a seasoned man with a no-nonsense attitude, listened intently, his curiosity growing by the minute.

"I see," he said, tapping his fingers. "And you believe this individual is a danger to national security?"

"Yes, Sergeant," John replied. "We have reason to believe he is involved in something far more sinister than simple trespassing. His interest in the Chapel and its connection to the Rosicrucian secrets could be a matter of grave concern."

The sergeant nodded, his eyes narrowing. "Very well, I'll release him into your custody. However, I would appreciate being informed of any developments. This is, after all, still my jurisdiction, and I won't have any funny business going on under my watch."

Eileen and John assured him of their cooperation, and with that, they were led to the holding cell where Albert was being detained.

John said, "Sergeant, would you excuse us, please?"

As Eileen stood there, taking in the sight of Albert, her mind raced back to the first time their paths had crossed aboard a double-decker bus. She recalled the moment vividly; the rain-specked window, the musty scent of wet umbrellas, and Albert's unexpected conversation. And now, there he was, a captive in a cell, his fate resting in their hands.

Albert spoke, his voice steady despite the surprise that flickered in his eyes. "Eileen Green, I presume?" he began, a hint of a smile playing at the corners of his mouth. "I recruited you into MI5, and I know all about your remarkable talents. Your ability to decipher codes and your math skills make you an invaluable asset. We needed your skills for a mission of utmost importance, and I knew that note would spark your curiosity."

Eileen's heart raced as she realized the extent of Albert's involvement in her life, the web of intrigue he had drawn her into. "You see, Eileen," Albert continued, "the Rosicrucian secrets we seek are not just ancient history. They hold the key to a powerful force that could change the course of this war. Our mission is to ensure those secrets don't fall into the wrong hands."

John interrupted, "I think we need a little more information as to what part you play in this, Mr. Schulte, before we continue."

Albert reached into his pocket and pulled out a small notebook. "Call this number, and it will clear things up for you." John left the cell and went back to the sergeant's office to make the call.

"My dear Eileen, I am pleased to meet you again. I'm also sorry to be the cause of you learning that your father, being a bit of a ladies' man, had several children out of wedlock. I'm one of those children, and therefore, your half-brother." Albert said, his eyes sparkling with a mixture of mischief and warmth. "You see, our family has a unique legacy, a connection to the ancient Rosicrucian secrets, and we tried on several occasions to include your father, Claude. He wasn't interested, being perhaps too busy elsewhere. Given your exceptional skills in code-breaking and mathematics, I wanted to find a way to involve you." Albert's voice was steady, and he exuded an air of confidence, as if he held all the cards.

119

Eileen stood there, her blue eyes narrowing as she took in this revelation about her father. She had always known her father to be a charismatic and adventurous man, but this was a side of him she had never considered. He had spent most of his working life as a pastry chef on the White Star ships and had been gone for months at a time.

The idea that she had several half-siblings was shocking, and she wondered how much her sister, Winnie, and brother Leslie knew.

"You knew about this, Albert?" she asked, her voice steady despite the turmoil of emotions she was feeling. "You knew about our father's secrets and never said a word?"

Albert's eyes held a mixture of apology and determination. "I have been a spy in MI6 for several years now, and I have been working undercover with a group of Nazi sympathizers. I've had little time to consider my personal life."

John came back into the room. "Well, Commander, after several calls and climbing the chain of command, I now understand the situation."

John's world had tilted on its axis as he processed the revelation that Albert Schulte, the man they'd been pursuing, was, in fact, an MI6 agent. Pieces of the puzzle began to fall into place, while at the same time, a myriad of questions sprang to mind. How had Albert ended up in MI6? And what role had he played in recruiting Eileen?

As if reading his thoughts, Albert addressed John directly, his expression a mix of contrition and resolve. "I know you must have a lot of questions, Mitchell. Let me explain how I came to be involved with MI6 and how our paths became intertwined with Eileen's."

Albert's gaze flickered, a fleeting shadow of uncertainty crossing his features. "It all started several years ago when MI6 approached me. They had been monitoring my activities due to my German heritage and suspected ties to Nazi sympathizers." Albert paused, his eyes hardening with determination. "I agreed to become a double agent, feeding misinformation to the Nazis and reporting their activities to MI6. It was a dangerous game, but one that I have played well since the 1930s and then one fateful day, I encountered you, Eileen, and noticed a crossword book in your uniform pocket. So it was our conversation about puzzles and your interest in ciphers that truly sealed the deal. I knew then that you would be a good candidate for MI5; so, I set up a series of clues that we published in the Daily Telegraph and purposely dropped notes, hoping you would pick up on the plan."

Eileen's curiosity about Albert's motives deepened as she listened. She knew her own recruitment story, but hearing it from Albert's perspective added a layer of intrigue. "And now here we are," she said, her voice steady. "Siblings, connected by more than just family ties. It seems our paths were always destined to intersect."

Albert's expression softened, and for a moment, the tension in the room eased. "Indeed, Eileen. Our family legacy has brought us together, and I am glad it did. The team at Bletchley are precisely what we need to unravel the Rosicrucian secrets and ensure they are protected from those who would misuse them. It's quite important, Mitchell, that after the time and effort I've spent to gain trust undercover, we continue to behave as though I'm under arrest and being taken to a military prison."

"I am sorry, sir, but that will mean you have to spend another night here. We will collect you in time for the morning train."

The next morning, the sergeant, true to his word, wasted no time in releasing Albert into the custody of John and Eileen. With a subtle nod, he indicated that they were free to leave.

Once outside the police station, with Albert in handcuffs, Albert turned to Eileen, "I must admit, I didn't expect you to chase me down in Rosslyn. Your talents never cease to amaze."

Eileen, her blue eyes flashing, replied, "Indeed, Albert. It seems our family ties run deeper than we thought. But make no mistake, I am well aware of your reputation and your penchant for secrecy."

"Fair enough. But rest assured, my allegiance lies with MI6, and I am here to aid your mission, not hinder it. We share a common goal: to protect the Rosicrucian secrets from falling into the wrong hands."

John, ever the pragmatist, cut to the heart of the matter. "Very well, Albert. We will brief you on our findings thus far, but first, we must return to our temporary base. There is much to discuss, and time is of the essence."

With a nod, Albert indicated his agreement, and the trio made their way over to Finlay, who was waiting to drive them to the train station.

14

Unlocking the Mystery

A s they settled back into the familiar surroundings of Hut 7 that evening, Eileen found a new teabag and made herself a cup of strong, steaming tea, her hands steady despite the whirlwind of emotions swirling within her. Albert declined the offer of tea, his eyes keenly taking in their makeshift headquarters. John wasted no time in filling Albert in on their progress, or lack thereof, with the mysterious device.

"Leonard," he said, handing the device to him, "explain to everyone what you have discovered so far."

With an uncertain look of frustration, Leonard responded, "We've hit a roadblock, I'm afraid. This device is unlike anything we've encountered before. What we have figured out so far is that we think it slides into a round slot, and when you turn the front six discs in a certain combination, the back corresponds, and that would, we think, may start the internal lock mechanism to open the door or device, just like a key opens a door."

Albert's keen interest was piqued, and his Nazi connections suddenly became relevant. "I may be able to offer some insight," he said cautiously. "My sources within the Nazi party have hinted at a similar device. It's said to be a key to something far more significant, but its true purpose remains unknown." Albert's double agent status hung in the air.

Eileen's curiosity got the better of her, and she probed further. "What exactly are these connections of yours, Albert? And why would they share such sensitive information?"

Albert's response was measured. "Let's just say I've cultivated relationships with individuals who value power above patriotism. They seek to use this device for their own gain, and I intend to use that to our advantage."

The unexpected arrival of Major Williams heightened the tension. He seemed surprised, yet also relieved to find Albert.

The major spoke up, "Have we made any progress in figuring out what the device is used for?"

"Well, Major, Leonard has a wealth of experience with safe combination locks, and I think we should concentrate our energy in that direction," Eileen remarked.

"Sounds good, Eileen. I'll leave you three to work things out. Don't hesitate to contact me if you need any additional help.

"Understood, sir."

After promising to get in touch if he found any information that might clarify their search, Albert left for the city, and the others had a late tea before finding their beds.

The next morning, Eileen caught up with the work the team had done while she was away.

"The discs. Intriguing," Leonard murmured. "It resembles an ancient combination key to a lock, yet the mechanism is far more complex. I suspect it may open some sort of cryptographic lock, designed to protect highly sensitive information."

"Do you have any more information that we could use?" Eileen asked Professor Richardson.

"Yes," said Professor Richardson. "I have a notebook from Rosslyn Chapel that belonged to my great-grandfather."

They knew that the information contained within those pages could be pivotal in their quest. The journal was filled with intricate sketches and coded annotations, detailing his own father's exploration of a hidden device that was part of the ritual stone circles scattered all over Britain. It was said to house a powerful secret, one that could turn the tide of the war. As he pored over the pages, a particular symbol caught his eye, a cryptic design that seemed to correlate with the mysterious device. Could this be the key to unlocking the device and the secrets it held?

15

The Mysterious Object

By late August, they were making gradual progress. They had managed to correlate the intricate disc patterns with a complex cryptographic algorithm, but the true challenge lay in determining the precise sequence required to unlock the vault device.

They decided to leave Leonard to work on decoding the device. Harry, James, and Professor Richardson returned to Rosslyn to dig out the object they'd found, taking care not to disturb the surrounding stones. They alerted Finlay and Angus to meet them at the train station and drive them to the ruins.

As they approached the site under the bright blue of a late summer sun, the scent of ancient earth filled the air. The task ahead seemed daunting as they surveyed the area, considering how large an excavation they needed.

They erected a tent and laid out all the tools and shovels. The team, led by Professor Richardson, began their careful excavation. Finlay and John lowered a crate containing tools and brushes, and they set to work, carefully brushing away dirt and debris, their eyes scanning the surroundings for any signs of the other small objects.

Days turned into a week, during which they were sometimes glad of the shelter of the tent. Finally, the team's efforts were rewarded. They had successfully uncovered the mysterious object, and now it towered before them, an imposing cylinder that measured three feet in diameter and six feet tall. The device, with its intricate patterns and cryptic nature, promised long-hidden secrets.

"Somehow, we need to transport this back to Bletchley and have the team examine it. I'll arrange transport. Maybe the movers can knock together another crate," said John.

"How are we going to lift it out of here?" Richardson asked.

"That's a good question," John said.

Angus spoke up, "Callum has a tractor, winches and chains that might work. I'll get in touch with him."

By noon the next day, the arrangements had been made. Callum turned up with a tractor and a steel tripod system for pulling out tree stumps. It took about an hour with several people under the supervision of Professor Richardson to set everything up and carefully put the chains and wood cribbing around the object.

"Ok," John yelled out. "Start to lift it."

Callum revved up the engine and put the motorized winch in gear.

"Steady."

It started to rise, and after about 15 minutes, it was up enough to guide over to the wooden cribbing. They gently set it down and started to examine it. It was completely sealed and had withstood being buried well.

John Mitchell, leaning against a nearby shovel, remained silent, his gaze intensely focused on the cylinder.

"Five generations my family's been on this land and never seen anything like it. Feels uncanny," said Callum.

Professor Richardson approached cautiously, his notebook already open. "The symbols... they're consistent with late 16th-century Rosicrucian iconography, but the style... it's... unconventional. There's an element of... what might be termed 'alchemical singularly' integrated. Fascinating."

Silence fell upon the group, broken only by the rustling of the wind through the nearby trees. The cylinder remained a mystery next to the freshly turned earth, quietly awaiting further investigation. The team stood in awe as the mysterious cylinder was carefully loaded onto the lorry, ready for its journey back to Bletchley Park.

Eileen, covered with dust from the excavation, couldn't hide her excitement. "I can't wait to see what this ancient artifact was used for. It's as if we've uncovered a piece of history that time forgot."

Angus, his suspicious nature momentarily forgotten, nodded in agreement. "Aye, this could be a game-changer. Those symbols are like nothing I've ever seen. We may have just stumbled upon something truly special."

As the lorry rumbled off, Finlay asked, "Do you think we've bitten off more than we can chew? I mean, what if this thing holds some ancient power we can't control?"

John replied, "We'll cross that bridge when we come to it, lad. For now, our priority is getting this artifact back to Bletchley intact. Who knows what secrets it holds or how they might aid us in the war effort."

The diverse group, united by curiosity and a sense of adventure, bid farewell to the ruins, unaware of the challenges and revelations that awaited them at their destination. Little did they know that their discovery would not only change the course of history but also forever alter their lives.

Callum and Finlay stayed behind to fill in the hole.

Angus drove Eileen and her colleagues to the station to catch the afternoon train.

16

Unveiling the Ancient Mysterious Object

The next afternoon, the lorry pulled up outside Hut 4, where Eileen, John, Professor Richardson and Leonard were waiting eagerly to unpack the artifact. They had prepared an area in the middle of the room with what equipment they could get on short notice and were eager to examine the device. They had returned with more than just information; they had uncovered a trove of hidden knowledge, a cache of secrets from the ruins, all of which could turn the tide of the war. As they shared their experiences and revealed the extent of their findings, the atmosphere buzzed with a mixture of excitement and hope.

With careful precision, they unveiled the large, cylindrical object, approximately three feet in diameter and six feet high, that they had retrieved. The object had been carefully wrapped and protected during transport, ensuring its safe arrival at Bletchley.

Eileen brushed away the remaining dirt and debris, revealing a sleek, weathered surface beneath. It seemed to absorb the light, reflecting a mysterious aura. Professor Richardson leaned in, his astute gaze taking in every detail.

"It appears to be made of bronze and possibly copper. I've never seen anything quite like it. The symbols etched into its surface are ancient, definitely Rosicrucian."

John stepped forward, "Let's try to decipher what these symbols mean," he suggested. "They could hold the key to unlocking the very purpose of this object."

Professor James Beattie entered the hut, pipe in hand. "Ah, I received word of your findings," he said. "Remarkable! This discovery could shed light on long-lost ancient knowledge."

The symbols, it seemed, held a hidden message, one that spoke of ancient power and knowledge. As they worked, the extent of their discovery began to unravel, and with it, a new sense of hope emerged. Then they noticed a small, round cap that seemed to be concealing something.

Richardson, touching ever so gently, pushed it, revealing a hole. "This looks interesting," he remarked. He picked up a small torch and shone it into the hole. "It seems about six inches deep, he remarked. "Leonard, hand me the disc device?" He picked it up off the bench and gave it to Richardson. Richardson carefully tried to insert it into the hole, pushing it slowly, and it was a perfect fit.

They had been working on it for days, trying to figure out what it could be used for.

"Could this device be a key of sorts?" Eileen asked, her eyes darting between the two objects.

"It would appear that way, Eileen," he said, his voice steady. Perhaps each disc holds a different code or instruction. Each disc could represent a different function or aspect of this ancient technology. We must decipher the symbols to understand their true purpose."

"Do you think the legends are true, Richardson? Could it be an ancient weapon that has been lost for generations?" Professor Beattie asked.

Richardson, his astute gaze taking in the reactions of everyone, smiled. "That, my friends, is what we are here to find out. With this device and the knowledge contained within these symbols, we may just unlock the mysteries of a long-forgotten secret society."

The team's collective excitement and anticipation hung heavy in the air as they prepared to delve deeper into the secrets of the ancient mysterious object and the device that seemed intricately linked to it.

Richardson took out the notebook that Bruce, the caretaker at the chapel, had given him and began to thumb through the pages to a part he had seen a few days earlier.

Richardson looked up and said, "Take a look at this, Eileen." Eileen looked at the page in question.

"This looks like a possible combination for something. Maybe it opens a panel on this thing," she remarked. Based on what it says here, we have what appears to be a weapon."

The notebook seems to describe a device that was created to help defend against invaders and protect the Rosicrucian order.

DEVICE NAME: Aether Harmonic Disruptor (A.H.D.)

Core Concept: A mystic-mechanical device created by a secret order of Rosicrucians in the early 1800s, said to harness the vibratory "Aether" field *(a hypothetical medium that was once believed to fill all of space and transmit light and other electromagnetic waves)* that connects all living things and machines. Operated through a symbolic cryptic key, the device tunes into cosmic frequencies to disrupt the internal equilibrium of enemy machinery—or even the mind.

WORKING MODEL DESCRIPTION

1. Physical Structure:
Main Body: A brass and iron cylinder encased in ornate Rosicrucian engravings and geometric inscriptions.

Input Key: The cryptic-style Rosicrucian key fits into a magnetic socket chamber at the centre of the machine.

Control Rings: 12 independently rotating rings on the key align to specific Rosicrucian symbols representing planetary frequencies or "spiritual tones."

2. Internal Mechanisms:
Crystal Resonator Core: At the heart is a beryl crystal, surrounded by copper coils, induction windings and tuning forks.
Magneto-Oscillators: Rotating gears inside generate vibrational fields based on the positioning of the cryptic symbols.
Ferrofluid Dampeners: Regulate oscillation harmonics to prevent feedback or self-disruption.

3. Operating Principle:
When the correct symbolic frequency sequence is entered on the key, the machine:
Activates vibrational harmonics tuned to the frequencies shown on the Rosicrucian diagram (solar spectrum, planetary harmonics).
Engages low-frequency magnetic pulses (infrasound & extremely low frequency radio waves)
Projects a directional field of disruptive vibratory energy outward through the top disc array

POSSIBLE EFFECTS

Short-Range Use up to (1000 ft.):
Causes machinery to stall, compasses to spin, and metal components to vibrate out of alignment.

Biological Impact:
Induces nausea, confusion, or fatigue in exposed targets—mimicking psychological disarmament.

Long-Range Use:
Distorts ambient electromagnetic fields, interfering with rudimentary communications or signals.

DECODING FUNCTION
The symbols on the key rings represent combinations of:
Planetary alignments (from the diagram)
Chords of the solar spectrum (the keyboard + element table)
Esoteric numbers (3, 7, 12)
Only one correct alignment configures the device to "resonate" with the targeted energy field.

SCHEMATIC INSPIRATION
The schematic is treated as a Rosicrucian master chart:
The sun and corona diagram represent the origin of energy.
The musical keyboard maps harmonics to physical vibration frequencies.
The solar spectrum shows tuning ranges.

Device Components
1. Cryptic Key Interface
A 12-ring golden cylinder, each ring engraved with Rosicrucian symbols.

Acts as the input system for frequency programming; each combination corresponds to a specific "vibrational mode." Rings must be aligned to unlock the internal harmonics. Incorrect sequences yield no effect or could cause a misfire.

2. Magnetic Resonator Core

A chamber within the engine houses:
Rotating rare-earth magnets embedded in concentric rings.
Ferro-magnetic rods aligned with the Leyden discharge plates.
An array of crystals (quartz and topaz) that focus magnetic pulses into vibratory beams.

3. Frequency Chamber

Powered by a pentagon Beryl crystal
Generates specific sonic frequencies matched to harmonic patterns from the diagram
Uses tuning forks aligned to the solar spectrum section on the schematic.

4. Aetheric Emitter Array

Consists of a blue beryl crystal inside the main body that, when activated, triggers circular crystalline rings that rise up to amplify and project the vibratory/frequency field, 2 to 10 ft in a 360° pattern from the unit.
This will deliver the harmonically disruptive energy to the target area.

Programming and Operation

The operator inserts the cryptic key and aligns the rings to match planetary symbols (Mercury through Pluto) from the solar system arc. Harmonic chords from the piano scale grid in the diagram.

Mineral codes (e.g., Barium, Vanadium) represent energy amplifiers.
Turning the key to the "initiated" position activates the device.
Turn the symbols in the opposite direction and pull the key out to disable the function

Cryptic Codes Effect

Discordant Pulse ⊙ ☿⊐†✳✳ Causes confusion, nausea, and mental fog in enemies.

Mechanical Null ☿ℏᛈ†✿ ☼ Disrupts gears, compasses, and mechanical targeting.

Aether Collapse ♀ ☿⊙†♅ Temporary paralysis or unconsciousness.

Cloak of Silence ☽⊐ℏ✳✳† silences the area acoustically used for stealth.

   Eileen's eyes widened in amazement as she studied the notes. The dimly lit room seemed to fade away as she focused on the words. Her gaze flicked back and forth, taking in every detail. As she finished reading, a look of determination settled on her face. She turned to her colleagues and spoke, her voice serious and resolute. "We need to proceed with caution."
   Just then, Major Williams came in to check on their progress. Looking at the artifact, he said, "So this is what all the noise is about. Everyone is waiting with bated breath to hear if you have made any progress."
   Richardson responded anxiously, saying, "It appears to be a weapon of some kind, and we are reluctant to test it inside."

Eileen then turned to the Major and asked, "Can we find a military testing facility to verify its effectiveness?" The gravity of the situation was evident in her intense gaze.

"I'll see what I can do." Major Williams left and went back to his office to inquire about a testing facility.

17

Unexpected Events

Major Williams' search for a testing ground led him to an abandoned airfield in Croydon, on the outskirts of London. It was the perfect location, with a separate entrance, offering ample space and privacy for their mysterious object. Lieutenant Coleman, with John Mitchell and Eileen, travelled the following day to the abandoned airfield. Their steps echoed across the deserted tarmac as they surveyed the space. It was the perfect venue for their mysterious object. Back at Bletchley, the team was about to uncover another piece of the puzzle. Their experimentation continued, each attempt bringing them closer to the truth hidden within the ancient object.

Coleman returned to Hut 4 to find Richardson suggesting they try a couple of the combinations that had been written down in the notebook. The team was apprehensive about trying that inside the hut, based on the potential outcome.

They gathered the next day at the abandoned airfield. Major Williams had ensured the artifact had been transported safely and that the area was secure. They carefully unloaded the artifact from the lorry and set it up on an old but smooth runway, surrounded by the eager group. Richardson and Eileen stood by, notebooks in hand, ready to record the outcome of this risky endeavour.

"Let's begin," Richardson announced, his voice steady despite the anticipation in the air. "Eileen, if you would be so kind as to enter the combination."

Eileen stepped forward, her hands steady as she carefully inserted the key and began turning the discs to the specified alignment. I'm using the setting - Mechanical Null ☿ ♄ ♇ ✝ ⚹ ☼, which should disrupt gears, compasses, and mechanical targeting."

As she adjusted the discs, a low hum emanated from the artifact, growing in intensity. The team watched, transfixed, as the object began to vibrate.

"It's working!" Richardson exclaimed, his voice filled with excitement. "Look at the seismograph readings!" The needles on the seismographs danced wildly, recording the vibrations emanating from the artifact.

"Incredible," Eileen murmured, her eyes shining with curiosity and excitement. "We've definitely unlocked something here, but what exactly have we unleashed?"

The team exchanged curious glances. Then the unit's top, an iris, opened, revealing the beryl crystal rising from the unit with five blue rings surrounding it. The instruments went off the scale as a visible coloured wave could be seen emanating from the crystal rings. All of their recording devices were being bombarded from all sides, and they weren't able to record anything but gibberish. Feeling a little dizzy, Eileen walked away from the unit as its intensity continued to grow.

"I think that's enough for now," said Lieutenant Coleman. "How do we shut it down?" Richardson said,

"According to the notes, you turn the symbols in the opposite direction and pull the key out to disable the function."

Eileen proceeded, and the Crystal with the rings began to descend slowly. The instruments began to settle down.

"This is extremely powerful, sir," John said, alarmed.

They wheeled the unit from the runway back inside the hangar.

"Well done, everyone," said Coleman, "I'll leave you lot to keep working things out. I'm going to head back to Bletchley."

They opened the iris again and started to examine the unit closely. They had brought as many tools and instruments as they could access to measure electrical, magnetic and vibrations, plus a portable, albeit very rudimentary X-Ray machine. After several days of examination, they had a couple of theories.

They believed that by harnessing the energy of hidden magnets, the device leveraged the resonant oscillations of beryl crystals. As the rings counter-rotated, precisely tuned tuning forks generated coherent frequencies, projecting focused vibrational waves and highly specific emissions beyond the unit's confines.

The team delved deeper into the mysteries of the artifact, their curiosity and determination fuelling their pursuit of answers. They discovered that the magnets and crystals were indeed integral to its power source, but the true enigma lay in the intricate interplay of frequencies and vibrations. Each disc, when turned, emitted a unique frequency, and when combined in specific alignments, they created a harmonic resonance that unlocked its secrets. But it was the reversal of this process that truly intrigued them. Richardson's discovery of the shutdown mechanism, dialling the symbols in the opposite direction, hinted at a deeper complexity, a sophisticated understanding of energy manipulation that defied their expectations of ancient technology.

As they continued their investigations, they encountered more challenges and surprises. The artifact's inner workings were unlike anything they had ever encountered, and they soon realized that their initial theories only scratched the surface of its true capabilities. Each discovery raised new questions, and they found themselves immersed in a labyrinth of ancient knowledge and power. The team's dedication and expertise were tested as they strived to unravel the artifact's mysteries, always mindful of the potential dangers that lurked within its ancient mechanisms.

The abandoned airfield became their sanctuary, a secluded arena where they could safely explore the artifact's power. Major Williams ensured their privacy, understanding the sensitive nature of the work. Every day, the team encountered more intricate mechanisms and hidden functions, each discovery building upon the last. The artifact seemed to hold an infinite number of secrets, and the team's excitement grew with each revelation. But with every answer, new questions arose, and they soon found themselves entangled in a web of ancient technology, where the boundaries of human understanding were constantly pushed and challenged.

They decided to try the other codes, but not before creating a fail-safe way to reach the unit without succumbing to its effects.

One of the lead scientists said, "If the unit relies on radio frequencies and high-range vibrations, then we need to create some shield to surround ourselves when approaching it. They got to work on a lead shield so that two soldiers could stand behind it and wheel it out to the artifact for protection.

They carefully moved the unit and placed it on the runway.

One of the scientists who specialized in chemical and physiological effects on humans decided to set up an experiment to test the effect of causing confusion, nausea, and mental fog in enemies. To do this, they had a soldier walk out to the unit, insert the key, and begin turning the discs to that combination in the notebook.

Discordant Pulse ⊙ ⚥ꝺ†✶✶ Causes confusion, nausea, and mental fog in enemies.

Right on cue, the unit began to hum, and the iris opened. The man was ordered to return to the hangar, but started to stagger as the vibrational waves seemed to interfere with his balance. His partner, inside the hangar, not yet overcome by the vibrational waves, ran out to rescue him, and the lead shield worked.

For several days, they repeated the experiment, recording how close a person could get to the device and how far away a person had to be to be unaffected. Then they worked on the shields to see how effective they were at various thicknesses and distances. A heavy shield would be cumbersome in battle; so, they tried other materials and configurations.

They spent almost a month considering the first setting and knew they had only scratched the surface. Major Williams, on one of his visits, suggested they move on.

Aether Collapse ♀ ☿☉✝♅ Temporary paralysis or unconsciousness.

One of the protection details walked out and inserted the key. He began to turn the discs to match the sequence. Nothing happened until he stood up and began to walk back. Then the unit came to life, and he struggled to move his body and fell. He yelled out that he was OK, but began having trouble breathing. Again, the lead shield was used for a rescue mission to disable the unit.

"Well, ladies and gentlemen, I think we have demonstrated that the artifact works as specified in the notes," Richardson said, "but I would still like to examine it further to find out if we can duplicate it. The team's excitement was palpable as they wheeled the artifact back into the hangar, eager to delve into its inner workings and uncover the secrets of its power.

The Professors' vast knowledge of ancient Rosicrucian cryptic symbols and history guided their efforts to understand the complex interplay of frequencies and vibrations. Together, they formed a formidable team, determined to unravel the ancient technology before them.

"But what else is the artifact capable of, and how do we discover other combinations?" Eileen asked.

Professor Beattie entered the hangar with the large book which he had received from McAllister. "I believe I may have stumbled upon something of interest," he said. "I believe we may be able to discover other symbols based on Chladni's technique, first published in 1787 in his book Entdeckungen über die Theorie des Klanges ("Discoveries in the Theory of Sound"), which consisted of drawing a bow over a piece of metal whose surface was lightly covered with sand. The plate was bowed until it reached resonance, at which point the vibration caused the sand to move and concentrate along the nodal lines, where the surface remained still, outlining the nodal lines. The patterns formed by these lines are now known as Chladni figures.

"Ok," Beattie said with enthusiasm. "What if we sprinkle some sand on the top of this, take a bow, and slide it down the side to see what shows up?"

"Where are we going to find a violin bow in an abandoned hangar?" asked Eileen.

"What if we could use our base radio to generate frequencies?" the young physicist asked.

"That's good thinking. Let's get the Lieutenant to set it up." Eileen replied.

The team gathered around the object. They started to dial the radio, but all it produced was static with no effect. Then, one of the scientists took a thin metal rod, placed it on the top rim of the unit, and touched the other end to the radio's metal case. It started to vibrate the sand, but didn't produce any significant patterns; so, they kept turning the dial, but to no avail.

Despite the initial disappointment, the team's curiosity was far from satisfied. Professor Richardson, his gaze intense, studied the sand patterns, his mind working through the possibilities. Perhaps there's a specific frequency we need to achieve. Let's not give up just yet." The team nodded in agreement. They began to discuss other methods. The object revealed its secrets slowly, but the team was persistent, driven by their fascination and a desire to understand.

Professor Richardson went back to the notes. "It states here that other functions would be revealed by placing it in the concentric circles inside the sacred place under the watchful eyes of the angels."

Richardson's query hung in the air. "Any insights, team?"

Eileen offered a tentative proposition: "The artifact's discovery within the ancient stone, a perfect circle, is significant."

John ignored her. "Further observations, anyone?"

Just then, Lieutenant Coleman arrived. "What's the status?"

Richardson's response was terse: "Stalled, sir. We require a series of nested circles to proceed."

Intrigued, Coleman pressed: "The basis for this hypothesis?"

Richardson explained: "The book's notes explicitly mention the concentric circles."

"Have you attempted the Chladni technique?" Coleman inquired.

Richardson's reply was disheartening: "Useless. It yielded no results."

Eileen, however, repeated her suggestion, her voice barely above a whisper.

Coleman, captivated, urged: "Enlighten us, Eileen."

"Sir," she began, her gaze resolute, "the only other circles —a long chance, I admit—are back at the ruins or maybe in the chapel. They may be worth investigating."

After a few moments of thought, the Lieutenant agreed and said, "If you are fairly certain, then transport it back to Rosslyn."

18

Into the Mystic, Challenges Await

E ileen Green, accompanied by Professors Richardson and Beattie, embarked on their journey back to the Rosslyn Chapel by train, leaving the artifact to follow by transport. They were all hoping the chapel, shrouded in legend, held the key to unlocking the secrets of the Rosicrucian artifact. They arrived very late, but Hamish found them a pot of tea and sandwiches before they settled into their rooms at the inn for the night. The next morning, it was raining, the cold drizzle of late October. They spent the morning by a fire studying their diagrams. They were grateful that after a light lunch, the rain slacked off a little before they walked to Rosslyn Chapel.

Bruce, the caretaker, greeted them. "It's delightful to see everyone again," was immediately followed by an introduction to Professor Beattie. Professor Richardson, a familiar face, received a courteous nod of acknowledgement along with Eileen.

Beattie started the conversation. "So far, our examination of the artifact suggests that finding out other functions might hinge on placing it within a series of circles in a specific area, possibly

147

the ruins? Does any detail of such a designated location resonate with you?"

"Not that I can recall," Bruce replied, but we can visit the ruins.

When they got there, Richardson was the first to comment, "Let's look around and see if we can find a spot that matches the notebook's description."

Half an hour of searching revealed no series of circles matching the description.

Bruce suggested they head back and look at the Chapel grounds and possibly inside the Chapel.

They searched the grounds to no avail. Then they ventured into the heart of the Chapel. Their eyes scanned the intricate carvings and symbols that adorned the walls, searching for any clues that could guide them. The symbolism seemed to be tied to a constant theme, but what was it?

For centuries, scholars and archaeologists alike had been trying to figure out the carvings. What was the purpose and meaning behind them? The mixture of Pagan and Christian symbolism, combined with other secret societies such as the Knights Templar and the Rosicrucians, created far more questions than answers.

"I have an idea," Bruce offered. "The circles you seek," he said, "I think lie within the heart of the sacred place, follow me."

There, etched into the stone floor, were three concentric circles, their precision striking. A hollow space beckoned at their centre. They suspected that within those circles lay the key to activating the artifact.

As the group was studying the circles, John arrived with his assistant and found the team in the chapel. "Where would you like us to place the artifact?"

"Over here, gentleman. We need to unpack the crate and do some measuring."

Professor Richardson took the lead and began measuring the artifact and the circles.

Much like a key sliding smoothly into a lock, the artifact effortlessly fit over the three circles on the floor. Richardson's suggestion to move it into place was met with eager agreement from the group.

"Now what?" Professor Beattie questioned.

"Well," said Richardson, "have you noticed the acoustics since we have been in this part of the chapel? Our voices have been echoing, and any sounds we make are reverberating."

"It's always been like that, in fact, there are a couple of spiritualists in town that often sit around the circles and chant," Bruce remarked.

"Let's put the sand on top of the artifact and try the Chladni effect with the bow, Richardson suggested. Beattie removed the bow from its case, and as Eileen moved the bow along the top ring, symbols began to appear.

"Perhaps it was designed to reveal its secrets only inside the chapel," Eileen said.

"Look at the symbols around the artifact and see if they match as I keep running the bow on the rim," said Richardson. "Amazing, these are matching up to the symbols in the notebook, and they coincide with certain frequencies."

Just then, Bruce interrupted and said, "Look at the ceiling; it's one of the symbols you just created".

As the group studied the symbols that appeared in response to the Chladni effect, Eileen's sharp eyes noticed something intriguing. Three of the symbols seemed to correlate with the notebook as musical notes: Middle C, A, and B. These notes, when translated into their corresponding frequencies, resulted in 261.2 Hz, 435 Hz, and 493.9 Hz, respectively.

With growing excitement, they began to consider the possibility of a sonic vibrational connection within the Chapel.

Eileen suggested they explore the Chapel's acoustics further. "Perhaps the ceiling carvings hold a clue to the frequencies we need to create," she proposed.

Professor Richardson proposed a solution. "Can we obtain the necessary equipment from Bletchley to generate precise frequencies and observe the artifact's reaction?" The group agreed and sent John back with a list, which included a request that a sound engineer to accompany him when he brought the equipment.

They posted a security detail at the Chapel, then left and went back to the inn. While eating dinner, they discussed the day's activities and began to formulate a plan to open the artifact and determine its operation.

Late the following day, the sound equipment and frequency generator, procured with the assistance of Major Williams, were set up in the chapel. They carefully positioned the artifact, ensuring the Rosicrucian symbols were aligned with the concentric circles etched into the chapel floor.

Eileen, her sharp eyes once again proving invaluable, noticed the intricate details of the vault key. She traced the intricate Rosicrucian symbols, understanding their role in unlocking the artifact's secrets.

As the sound equipment hummed to life, the team directed specific frequencies through a steel rod laid on the unit's edge and attached to the frequency generator.

The Chladni effect, visible in the sand, revealed vibrating symbols that matched those embedded in the artifact. Eileen's hypothesis proved correct; the chapel's acoustics played a crucial role in unlocking the mystery.

The team gathered around the artifact, their eyes fixed on the sand as the sound frequency generator began to work. Eileen, her sharp eyes never wavering, noticed subtle shifts in the sand's patterns with each change in frequency. John, ever attentive, observed her reactions, knowing her insights were crucial to their quest. The sound engineer, his finger on the generator's dial, methodically adjusted the frequency, his eyes flicking between the sand and the symbols adorning the artifact.

As the frequencies climbed, the sand began to dance, forming intricate patterns that seemed to echo the symbols surrounding them. A faint hum filled the chapel, resonating with an otherworldly quality.

Bruce, the caretaker, had an unreadable expression and stood slightly apart, his eyes darting between the artifact and the expectant faces of his companions.

Eileen's breath quickened as she noticed the sand forming a distinct pattern, one that seemed to mirror the vault key she had studied so intently. She leaned forward, her eyes narrowing in concentration. "I believe I see something," she said, her voice steady despite the excitement that gripped her. "The sand seems to be forming a shape akin to the key. It's as if the two are in dialogue."

They all looked on in astonishment, wondering what would happen next. Professor Richardson suggested inserting the key to see if matching the symbols forming on the top would have an effect. Eileen carefully inserted the key, and it stopped at the blank disc, allowing the remaining six discs to be turned clockwise.

As Eileen turned the discs based on the frequencies that the sound engineer was creating in combination, the team realized the sheer number of potential combinations was daunting. They needed to find a way to narrow down their options. Studying the intricate Rosicrucian symbols inscribed on the artifact and the surrounding chapel, they began to search for clues that could guide them in their quest to unlock its secrets. Each symbol seemed to hold a hidden meaning, a piece of a puzzle that, when assembled, might just reveal the purpose and function of the artifact key.

Eileen's sharp eyes once again proved invaluable as she noticed subtle connections between the symbols. Eileen began to dial in frequencies based on her instincts and the team's growing understanding of the chapel's acoustics. With each attempt, the sand danced and shifted, forming patterns that seemed to echo the fabric of the mystery they sought to unravel. However, the artifact remained stubbornly inert, offering no clues as to the correct combination.

Richardson, his archaeological instincts kicking in, suggested a new approach. "Let's focus on a symbol that is common to both the artifact and the notebook, as well as the sand symbols that appear in response to specific frequencies." The team nodded in agreement, recognizing the logic in his words. They began to scrutinize the intricate Rosicrucian symbols, searching for a common thread that could provide the elusive clue they needed.

Eileen suggested, "What if we try matching the frequencies to the symbols on the artifact and the notebook, and see if the sand responds in kind?"

Richardson's face lit up with excitement as he realized the potential of her idea. "Brilliant! We can use the frequencies as a sort of key, each one corresponding to a specific symbol. It's like trying to crack a safe, each number bringing us one step closer to opening the lock."

The team leaned forward, their eyes fixed on the artifact. With each turn of the discs, they felt they were one step closer.

Then, a breakthrough. As they matched the frequencies to the first symbol, the artifact emitted a soft hum, and the sand formed a pattern that mirrored the intricate design of the vault key. The sound engineer, his curiosity piqued, placed a stethoscope against the outer shell, and they all heard a faint, mechanical whirring sound from within. It was as if something was turning, activating hidden mechanisms deep within the artifact's heart.

Eileen's heart raced as she realized the significance of their discovery. "It's responding to the frequencies," she said, her voice filled with a mixture of excitement and awe. "It's as if the symbols are a code, and we've finally found the right combination."

John nodded in agreement. "We're getting closer," he said. "But we need to keep going. There's still more to uncovering the mystery."

As the team delved deeper into the chapel's mysteries, Bruce, the caretaker, made a startling observation. He noticed something amiss. "Look up, lads," he said, his voice echoing in the cavernous space. "The ceiling carvings have symbols that match those in the notebook and on the artifact. Could they be more than just decorative?"

Richardson and Beattie followed his gaze and spotted a cherub, its wings spread, perched atop a column directly above the concentric circles. "Indeed, Bruce," Richardson mused, "that is what was written in the notes, and it appears to be playing notes on a scale. A celestial hint, perhaps?"

Beattie added, his eyes narrowing in concentration. "A long shot, but worth considering. Let's see if we can decipher the notes and their correlation to the frequencies we've been experimenting with."

Eileen noticed something else intriguing. "The cherub's position," she said, her voice steady. "It's directly above the artifact when we place it on the circles. Could there be a connection between the notes it seems to be playing and the frequencies we need to unlock the artifact's secrets?"

John nodded in agreement. "It's worth investigating. We've come this far, and the chapel's acoustics and symbols have already proven crucial. Let's see if we can uncover the meaning behind the cherub."

As they studied the cherub, its wings spread wide as if embracing the very notes it played. Richardson suggested, "Let's try something." He looked at the sound engineer, "If you could dial in the frequencies corresponding to the notes the cherub seems to be playing, we might just strike the right chord, so to speak."

The engineer adjusted the frequency generator, and the sound filled the chapel. As the frequencies resonated, the sand began to dance, forming patterns that seemed to echo the cherub's melody.

The team's excitement grew as they witnessed the artifact's response to their efforts and as they carefully turned the discs on the key, matching the patterns that formed in the sand. Each turn of the disc corresponded to the frequencies generated by the sound equipment, creating a symphony of sorts that echoed throughout the chapel. After carefully aligning all six discs, the artifact began to respond slowly. The Iris on top began to open, emitting a soft mechanical sound, and the team could see the inner workings of the device—a series of rings and gears that turned in opposite directions in response to the frequencies.

They had unlocked some of its secrets, and now the question was whether it would function outside the chapel. They removed the key, and the artifact immediately closed.

19

The Weapon and
How They Deployed It

I t was late in the day when Angus came into the chapel.

"Hello, Angus," said Bruce. "What brings you by this evening, my friend?"

"I've found some other notes describing a meridian line that seems to join the circle in the ruins, where we discovered the device, and several other circles that have been discovered travelling south through Scotland and England. I think it's worth looking into because it describes activating the other circles by using the key."

Everyone looked stunned.

Angus's ancient notes revealed that the artifact was not just a standalone weapon but a part of a larger network. The device, it seemed, could communicate with other circles located throughout Scotland and England. Activating the circles with the cryptic key could potentially unleash a force unlike anything they had ever imagined.

Angus began to tell them what he had uncovered. "I was looking for some files in an old chest and came across an unmarked diary of my great-grandfather. He wrote about his everyday activities, which were very much the same thing every day; he was 17 at the time. Except one entry stood out as being very unusual. He was very interested in history and was exploring the ruins, which a lot of the kids did back then. There were tall tales of ghosts and strange occurrences that made their way into the village's folklore. He was out exploring one day near the ruins with his friend Andrew. It was dusk when they had a strange feeling come over them that they couldn't explain, and in the distance, looking towards the ruins, they could see a strange blue glow; so they decided to investigate it further. As they came over the hill, they saw blue circles floating above the ground and a blue crystal-like structure rising up in the centre. They also observed several men in robes chanting and holding rods, and one of them was reading from a book. He said they were not able to get closer because they started to feel sick, so they turned around and headed back home. When he and Andrew arrived home, their parents scolded them and said emphatically that they were never to go near the ruins again. That was the last time it appeared in the diary.

"That's incredible," said Professor Beattie.

"Indeed," said John. "On that note, I suggest we call it a day and regroup in the morning to move the artifact to the ruins."

The next morning, everyone returned to the chapel, and the team carefully packed up the artifact to transport it to the ruins. Then they looked to Angus to see if he had discovered any key combinations in his great-grandfather's notes that would activate the device. He had not. "There were references," he said, "to rituals that took place on certain dates. The members of the order would get together at the circle of *léargas spioradálta,* which is Gaelic, meaning 'spiritual enlightenment.' They developed the device as a means of defence for Scotland, and they would first meet at the chapel to obtain the codes that activated the Aether Harmonic Disrupter. There is no reference as to where the codes were in the chapel."

"Well, at least we've narrowed it down to the Chapel," said Richardson.

Eileen said, "If we are looking for something that would be used to possibly defend or ward off what they thought was the enemy, then we should be looking for a phrase or symbol of strength," she said.

Then Bruce remembered the words carved above the door leading to the vault.

"Dion Alba le ro-shealladh dìomhair," Angus said, "Defend, ye, Scotland by mystic providence. Now we have to find Rosicrucian symbols that match this, and even then, we don't know if that's the sequence for the key."

Richardson had brought his book on Rosicrucian mythology and started to look up the words.

Suddenly, Eileen's sharp eyes caught sight of a faint outline above the doorway. Brushing her fingers over the stone, she revealed a hidden compartment. Inside was an ancient parchment, its edges frayed with age. Unrolling it carefully, they discovered a series of intricate Rosicrucian symbols, the missing codes. They still weren't certain these would activate the device, but they had to try.

They made their way back to the ruins with anticipation in every step. The team carefully unloaded the artifact and installed it in its original resting place.

"Eileen, would you like to do the honours, seeing you discovered the symbols?"

With a slight tremble in her hands, she inserted the key and entered the sequence. The device started to hum. The magnetic resonator core thrummed, and the frequency chamber emitted a soft, resonant tone. It was as if the artifact was awakening, connecting to a power source beyond their comprehension. Eileen stepped back and watched in anticipation with the others.

The iris was not opening this time, but the rows of symbols etched around the device were starting to move in a circular pattern, and each one was moving in the opposite direction to the one above and below it. It was moving at quite a pace, and a hint of blue was emanating from between each circle. They watched it for about an hour, taking notes, but there didn't seem to be any measurable effect coming from it, so they turned it off. After some discussion, they decided to call it a day, assign a security detail to the area and make their way back to the Inn.

The next morning, they met for breakfast to plan. Hamish, the innkeeper, came over to the table to welcome everyone, and he looked at John, "A telegram came through this morning for you, John."

"The only people who know where we are are the Secret Service." John read it and looked up at everyone. "We have to go back to the ruins and turn on the device at 11 am."

"What's going on, John?" Richardson asked.

"I can't say right now with everyone around, but I'll inform everyone on the way back." With that, they finished a hearty breakfast and headed out. As soon as they arrived at the ruins, John informed everyone that MI5 and the secret service experienced some unexplained activity from their ground sensors."

"Sensors?" Eileen asked.

"Yes, the British government's geological survey has seismic sensors installed all over Britain and Scotland that report any activity on a 24-hour basis. They said they had some very strange readings yesterday afternoon, the same time the device was turned on. It seemed to be coming from the "Belinus Line.""

Richardson interrupted. "That is believed to connect sacred sites, including stone circles, across Britain and Scotland. This line is thought to represent a north-south axis of energy and power, with various landmarks and ancient sites positioned along it."

"It's almost 11 am," John reminded everyone, and we need to be ready, people."

At precisely 11 am, John signalled to turn on the device. They kept it running for 30 minutes as instructed, then shut it down. The security detail had a shortwave radio that enabled them to stay in contact with MI5 in London. The radio signal was plagued by excessive noise, making it difficult to understand. However, they were still able to record faint seismic readings coming from various locations in and around the immediate area, as well as from as far away as Glasgow and Newcastle.

The major ordered everyone back to Bletchley.

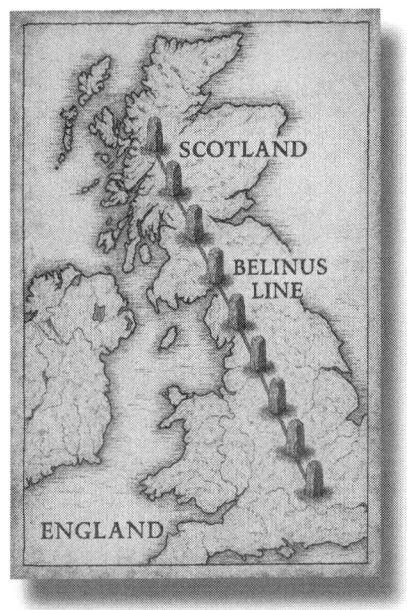

20

A Possible Chain
of Artifacts

The train ride back for Eileen, John, Professor Beattie, and Professor Richardson was intense, with more questions than answers. Despite the miserable weather, they were very excited and couldn't wait to share their findings.

The rain, which had begun not long after they left Edinburgh and followed them all the way south, showed no signs of letting up as the group arrived back at Bletchley. The journey had been a blur of excitement and speculation, and now they were eager to delve deeper into their discovery.

Eileen, John, and the professors stepped into the warm, bustling headquarters and made their way to the debriefing room, where they would present their findings. As colleagues and peers gathered to hear their report, the room was abuzz with anticipation.

They all took turns relaying their experiences and observations, painting a picture of the device and its incredible potential to the team of scientists, cryptographers and naval personnel. They talked for some time, and everyone took notes, trying to piece everything together and form plans to move forward. Arthur was very keen to try out other codes at the abandoned airfield and possibly set up a lab in one of the hangars.

As they were talking, the head of security knocked on the door, "Sir, you might want to look at this."

"What is it?" he said impatiently.

"I have a copy of today's *Daily Mirror*, and on page eight, there is a story about several people experiencing strange vibrations coming from their local stone circles."

"Thank you," Arthur said, and he took the paper from him. "What do you suppose this is all about?"

Both professors began reading the article and came to the same conclusion. The stone circles must be connected in some way.

Arthur said, "It might be an idea to send a team to each circle in question and see if there are other devices buried at each one. Eileen, why don't you and Beattie go to Glasgow, and John, you and Richardson can go to Newcastle."

"Great idea," said the Lieutenant, "This is definitely worth looking into."

The team assembled the next morning, with excitement and anticipation in the air. John and Professor Richardson joined the rest of the team as they loaded the equipment into the lorry for the twelve-hour journey to Newcastle.
Everyone was dressed for the unpredictable northern weather. November had long, dreary days with frequent rains, and when the team arrived in Newcastle, the sun was a mere memory, obscured by grey skies. The lorry rumbled to a stop, and they disembarked, stretching their legs and taking in their new surroundings. They were met by Daniel, the local MI5 operative, a man of medium build with a serious expression, his dark hair slicked back. He greeted them with a nod, his eyes alert and keen.

John shook Daniel's hand firmly. "Good to meet you, Daniel. We're eager to get started on this investigation." This is

Professor Richardson from the University of Edinburgh, an expert in ancient ruins.

"Pleased to meet you both," Daniel acknowledged.

They set off towards the stone circle, a mysterious and ancient site that held the promise of hidden secrets. As they approached, the circle loomed larger, the stones standing sentinel, silent guardians of forgotten knowledge. Daniel led them to the spot where the unusual vibrations had been reported.

"It happened right about here," Daniel said, his voice low and gravelly. "Local residents reported feeling strange vibrations, almost like a hum, that seemed to emanate from beneath the ground." John and Professor Richardson exchanged a glance.

As the team unloaded their equipment in the misty Newcastle air, Daniel was very curious about their mission. John filled him in on a need-to-know basis. "I'm afraid it's Top Secret, and we need your help in keeping this under wraps. If the locals find out, it could jeopardize the research."

"That's taken care of. We created a cover-up about a small seismic event, and the local newspaper published a short article about it."

"Well done. Thank you."

They began scanning the circle with their metal detector for evidence of the type of artifact they had found at Rosslyn. It didn't take long to uncover a device. They found it buried beneath the ancient stone circle. It was a duplicate of the Rosicrucian artifact. They dug it up, carefully extracted it from the earth, and cleaned it up for transport back to Bletchley. They had brought along packing material and a crate, hoping it was close to the same size as the original. This artifact fit perfectly because it turned out to be an exact duplicate of the one they already had. This raised more questions than answers.

What was its purpose? How long had it been buried? How many other similar artifacts are buried in the hundreds of stone circles scattered across the British Isles?

Meanwhile, Eileen and Professor Beattie had taken the train from Bletchley to Glasgow.

They arrived at the Stone Circle site and met Robert, the local MI5 contact, a man of few words with a no-nonsense attitude, greeted them. He briefed them on the situation, explaining that the vibrations had been felt by locals precisely when the Rosslyn artifact was activated. Eileen's curiosity grew as she imagined the potential link between the two events. They unloaded their equipment and began scanning the circle with their metal detector for evidence of another artifact, but came up empty.

However, based on the reports of seismic vibrations, they decided to dig with hand shovels in the immediate area and found an object, but it was not metal; it was a smaller ceramic device. As they carefully exhumed it, it began to reveal similar Rosicrucian symbols, but the keyhole was missing. They also had brought along packing material and a crate to transport it. After a long day of exploration, digging and packing, the crew left for Bletchley, while John and Eileen had made reservations for an overnight stay before returning once again to Bletchley.

21

The Unexpected Journey

Meanwhile, Albert had kept an eye out for any rumours that his Nazi connections were making progress on finding the artifact or developing a similar technology. All was quiet for months; then news arrived based on the stolen diagram from Hamish's cabinet.

Telegram: News of diagram-stop contact me stop.

Hamish explained when Albert got him on a secret line that he had found a note in his desk drawer. The note came from an unlikely source, Alex, a former employee from the inn in Rosslyn. It seemed that Alex's father was one of the people seen often at the ruins. He had grown up in Rosslyn, but his father was German, a machinist who had come to Scotland before World War I. The message was simple. *My father somehow knew about the cabinet and insisted I break in one night and steal the hidden diagram. Meet me at the train station alone. Tomorrow at 7 pm.*

Albert instantly contacted Lieutenant Coleman, who was excited that the bait they had left was finally leading them to their enemies. He agreed that Albert must be at the train station the next night.

The next evening was dark and damp, the evening mist hung low, and the last train had left, which meant the station master had closed for the day.

Albert approached the station, and Alex appeared out of the darkness.

"Alex?"

"Yes, I have some alarming news about my father and his friends."

Albert pointed to a seat in front of the station. "Sit down and tell me what you know. I'm here to help you."

Alex looked around and nervously started to tell him. "I think my father is a Nazi. I gave him the diagram a number of weeks ago, and his friends are helping him to figure it out. They are all skilled craftsmen and very intelligent, but they are also heavy drinkers, and they tend to talk too much. I have heard them at the pub saying they have figured out it's a weapon, and they are trying to make it work. If they are successful, they want to sneak it back to Germany. People in the pub think they are a joke, but I know about the stolen diagram, which might mean their boasting is true."

"Do they have a place where they are working on it?"

"Yes, I can take you there, but you have to promise me you'll protect me because I think he would kill me if I knew I had told someone."

"I need to scope it out first to determine the risk," Albert said.

Alex said, "I'll give you the address. You'll be able to figure it out from there. Yeah?"

"Agreed," Albert said, taking out a notebook and writing down the address. "If I need you, I'll leave a message with Angus."

166

When Alex had been gone for five minutes and the silence around the station was interrupted only by the sound of his own breathing, Albert joined up with the local MI5 man who had been hiding inside the station. They decided that no time was better than the present to look at the address Alex had given him. It turned out to be the old gunpowder mill. Alex had said to look for a small machine shop along the path and across the bridge.

The mill had been a going concern during WWI, but by World War II, the location was deemed too vulnerable to German air raids; so most of the equipment had been moved to Westcott and Summerfield to maintain safety and a continuous supply. Alex's father, Herman, was a machinist who had remained in the original factory area during the war to keep the remaining machines and their parts as needed. It was a perfectly hidden front.

Albert and his companion rode by the shop that night. They were unable to make out much because of the blackout curtains; there definitely was someone there. A motorbike and a couple of bicycles leaned against the wall near the door, and tiny slivers of light showed around the boarded-up windows.

Albert reported the next day to Bletchley. He and Coleman discussed the best way to use the traitors and their work. When they got off the secure line, Coleman and Williams continued the discussion. Williams had connections to Special Operations, but they were not available for such small missions. It was decided to have Albert go exploring at the gunpowder factory and gather more information.

Albert got in touch with Alex to see what his father's work schedule was, and they were in luck. A shipment of parts was expected the following afternoon. Albert made plans to intercept the package, disguise himself, and deliver the parts. He left late because Alex said they started drinking at around teatime and were drunk most nights.

After dark the next afternoon Albert, on a borrowed motorcycle with a large side car pulled up outside the factory and knocked on the door.

Herman answered, "You're late."

"I'm new to this route and I got lost."

"Well, come in and put the crate over there. Would you like a drink?"

"Don't mind if I do," Albert responded.

Alex was right, the men were drunk and loud. Albert looked around and said, "You've got quite the operation here. My father is a machinist, but his shop was sequestered for the war. I grew up with the smell of oils and metal."

"That's wonderful, laddie, now let me show what we're working on for the war effort," said Herman. He led him into the back room while the others told jokes and stories, entirely oblivious to Albert.

Herman pulled a large tarp off a strange-looking object. "That's peculiar," said Albert, surprised at what he saw.

"This is a special device that will end the war," said Herman.

Albert refused a second drink, with the excuse that he had more deliveries to make and drove to Edinburgh to report in with Coleman.

After he had described the inside of the factory and the men working there, he said, "What I glimpsed under the tarp was alarming, and I would like to know more about the fake diagram you constructed."

"Well, Commander, it was a fictional model for a type of electrostatic bomb. We had to make it look like the original Rosicrucian diagram with crystals and magnets, etc., but it was missing so much information that it would never work. I'm surprised they even have a prototype. The engineer who created it would be surprised, too."

168

"Whatever it is, I think we need to capture the device and bring them all in for questioning. In addition to their seditious talk, I also noticed several Nazi symbols pinned up on the board with what looked like the fake diagram," said Albert.

"Not so fast. If the thing they have built will never work, it may be better to let them keep busy with it and see who they contact. I'll report to Major Williams and see what he thinks. It's MI5's responsibility to combat enemy espionage. Williams may want to contact his counterpart at Redford barracks in Edinburgh and make a plan to watch this bunch."

22

The Dutch Connection

Two weeks later, Albert Schulte knocked on Arthur's door. He reported that he had heard rumours from his Nazi connections on the continent that they were questioning Jan van Rijckenborgh, a Dutch-born mystic, head of the Rosicrucian order in Holland.

"With your permission, Lieutenant," Albert suggested, I would like to delve into this and see if my operative in Holland could contact Jan van Rijckenborgh to see if he has any knowledge of the artifact."

"Good idea, Albert. Report back as soon as you can," Arthur Coleman responded.

Albert was able to find where Jan van Rijckenborgh, was being held outside of Amsterdam.

The Netherlands had surrendered on May 10, 1940, and this was late in 1941. Trying to get anyone out of Holland at the time was fraught with danger. Fake passports and documentation, in addition to travel arrangements, were required to make sure Jan didn't arouse any suspicion. Albert and his contacts in Holland arranged for van Rijckenborgh, with a bundle of recent and historical Rosicrucian literature that might help explain how the artifact worked, to escape and travel to the Hague, where he was picked up by an MI6 vessel disguised as a fishing boat and brought safely across the English Channel. The journey across the Channel was rough. In late autumn, the weather was nasty, and they dodged U-boats and the Kriegsmarine who were on constant patrol looking for defectors and smugglers.

Albert met Van Rijckenborgh who was seasick and exhausted. He welcomed him when he landed and accompanied him to Bletchley. The next day, Major Williams assembled everyone in Hut 7 to show Van Rijckenborgh what they had discovered.

As the group gathered in Hut 7, Albert introduced van Rijckenborgh who had risked his life to escape to Britain with his trove of recent Rosicrucian literature. He looked at the artifact, amazed. The artifact was well documented in the Rosicrucian literature but he'd never expected to see it. Using his expertise in ancient writings and esoteric knowledge, he began to confirm what the team had already been able to find and explain the purpose and power of the object though he had never seen it or witnessed the unit's capabilities.

"How did you find the artifact?" he asked.

Major Williams said, "Mitchell, why don't you take the lead on this?"

"Well, we started intercepting radio transmissions from Albert that seemed to indicate the Nazis had infiltrated northern Scotland and were looking for a secret weapon of some kind."

Albert interrupted to explain about one of the projects that the Nazis were working on in Germany. One of his connections regularly reported on the Nazi high command's unsettling fascination with the esoteric and occult. Their interest had been a subject of a hushed conversation at a lavish soirée hosted by Heinrich Himmler himself, a gathering Albert's contact had inadvertently overheard. MI6 operatives had questioned many people they knew who had connections to secret societies such as the Freemasons and the Rosicrucians. Himmler had created several squads to investigate, and one of them had found a rumour that there was a Rosicrucian weapon of enormous power, maybe somewhere in Scotland. Albert explained that he had immediately begun investigating the story.

"I shared the information with Eileen and John, which led to a fact-finding mission. I couldn't let on for some time that I was part of MI6 because that would have compromised the whole operation."

Van Rijckenborgh listened intently as the team filled him in on their knowledge of the artifact and their encounters with the Nazis' occult interests. His eyes widened at the mention of Scotland and the Rosicrucian weapon.

"I fear the Nazis may indeed be onto something," he said gravely. "There is a legend within the Rosicrucian Order of a powerful artifact, an ancient relic with immense mystical energy. It is said to bestow its owner with incredible power, and its existence has been a closely guarded secret for centuries." Jan paused, his eyes flicking to the artifact. "I have only ever seen illustrations and read vague descriptions in ancient texts. But I believe this may be the very object the Nazis are seeking."

The room fell silent as the weight of this revelation sank in.

Major Williams spoke first, his voice steady. "Can you tell us more about it, Van Rijckenborgh? What are its origins, its powers, and most importantly, how can we use it against the Nazis?"

Van Rijckenborgh nodded, his expression determined. "I will share everything I know. The Rosicrucian Order has studied and protected this knowledge for generations. It is our duty to ensure it does not fall into the wrong hands."

And so, over the next several hours, Van Rijckenborgh delved into the artifact's ancient history and mystical properties. He explained its origins, tracing it back to a secret brotherhood that existed long before the Rosicrucians. The team listened, captivated by the tale of a device that could harness and amplify the power of the Earth's vibrational frequencies, a tool that could be used for incredible good or unspeakable evil. As the sun set outside Hut 7, they began to piece together a plan not only to keep the artifact out of Nazi reach but also to use it as a weapon against them.

"Could I see it in action?" van Rijckenborgh asked.

"Yes," Said Major Williams, "but we have to transport it to a clandestine location we have set up for testing."

"Let's call it a day, people. Jan, we've arranged accommodations for you. We will meet first thing tomorrow morning."

"Before we retire, I'm curious," asked John. "Are there any Rosicrucian members in Scotland who could have helped us?"

"Yes, and no," said Jan. "They wouldn't have access to this knowledge. Only the elders understand this side of the teachings, and the only Rosicrucians who are presently here are not elders. They don't advertise their existence, so you would have compromised the entire project by asking around or putting an ad in a local paper, for example."

That evening, Major Williams had the unit transported to the airfield along with other testing equipment.

The next morning came quickly and was met with excitement and anticipation.

Both Professors arrived along with Eileen, John, Jan and Albert.

The security team and the engineers had already set up the device on the runway and were ready to test the existing codes. They had predetermined the code:

Mechanical Null ☿ℏ℮✝✿ ☼ Disrupts gears, compasses, and mechanical targeting.

A security detail accompanied Eileen and Jan out to the device, and Eileen inserted the key. "Would you like to dial a combination, Jan?"

"It would be an honour, Mrs. Green." The team watched in awe as the device sprang to life, its intricate mechanism whirring and buzzing. The five rings rose gracefully, emitting a soft hum that seemed to vibrate through the atmosphere. They had planned for an aged surplus jeep to approach from behind the hangar, and as it did, it seemed that everyone stopped breathing, knowing this was the true test. The vehicle sputtered and stalled, its engine failing as it drew near the artifact. Cheers erupted from the group, and even van Rijckenborgh, usually stoic, couldn't contain his excitement.

"Unbelievable!" he exclaimed. "I have studied the Rosicrucian teachings for decades, but to see this ancient power manifested so tangibly is beyond my wildest dreams."

They were able to get close enough to the device to look inside at the mechanism and try to determine how it might be generating the frequencies. They had brought along a 16mm film camera to film the device in action. It had a hand crank to safeguard against the artifact's energy pulse.

The team's excitement over the results of the test was short-lived as they remembered the grave threat the Nazis posed.

Major Williams broke the optimistic mood. "While this demonstration is encouraging, we must remember that our enemy is relentless in their pursuit of power. We cannot afford to let our guard down. Van Rijckenborgh, your expertise is invaluable, and we would be honoured if you would continue to aid us in this endeavour."

Van Rijckenborgh nodded solemnly. "Of course, Major. I am committed to ensuring this artifact does not fall into Nazi hands. I will do everything in my power to assist you in understanding and harnessing its full potential."

With a sense of renewed purpose, the team dispersed for the evening, each member lost in their thoughts about the artifact and the role it could play in the war.

In the coming days, they developed the film and viewed it together to determine how the unit actually functioned. They discovered the beryl crystals were the key to the operation. When the combination key was inserted into the keyhole, it seemed to activate the internal magnetic rings which surrounded the crystal, and a magnetic suppression of buoyancy convection was detected. This seemed to generate a convection effect that, in turn, radiated the vibrations and frequencies based on the dialled key combinations.

The Major was able to convince the War Office to release funding for the project.
In the following days, vehicles arrived with additional supplies to establish a lab and living quarters at the airport. Among the supplies were the two unearthed artifacts from Glasgow and Newcastle. They were carefully cleaned by Richardson and van Rijckenborgh, who were amazed that they had located two more units. They got to work examining them to see if they were similar. Van Rijckenborgh had found in his notes that the keys to activate the units were individually crafted when they were constructed, but there was also a way to create a master key that supposedly activated additional units. This left a big question: how to create a master key.

Van Rijckenborgh was able to determine that the ceramic one was a type of capacitor, which meant it received energy from the other metal units to boost the transmission to other buried units, so he began researching the master key theory.

Through meticulous examination of Rosicrucian texts and manuscripts, aided by Eileen's knowledge and van Rijckenborgh 's expertise, they unearthed arcane symbols. These enigmatic markings revealed a pivotal insight: a master key could be forged by cleverly manipulating the initial four discs, aligning them with the master symbols, thus unlocking previously inaccessible secrets.

Jan and Eileen presented the findings to the team, and they all agreed to test it out on the newly acquired metal artifact from Glasgow. They took it out to the runway and set it up to activate it using the Mechanical Null combination.

Initially sluggish, the unit sputtered to life. Minutes later, the iris unfurled, revealing the five concentric rings. Appearing functional, it then catastrophically failed, collapsing before their eyes. Remarkably, the iris remained stubbornly open, radiating a chilling absence of power. They retreated back to the hangar with the unit in tow, and after a meticulous examination, revealed the devastating truth: the beryl crystal, the heart of the system, had fractured, rendering the unit utterly useless.

Major Williams convened a meeting to determine the next steps. The discussion centred around dismantling the unit to find out exactly what it was made of and how it worked.

The days ahead were very challenging. They determined that the composition of the outer casing was bronze, and the inside components were brass. The magnetic rings were unusual because they were sandwiched between two metal plates of iron, which focused and reinforced their magnetic flux lines. When the key was inserted, it caused the large rings to move in opposite directions and start spinning around the crystal, creating the vibrational frequencies.

Progress and Setbacks

The team's painstaking work paid off as they uncovered the inner workings of the ancient machine. Each day brought new discoveries as they carefully took the machine apart, documenting every gear, lever, and symbol. By the autumn of 1943, they realized that the machine was far more complex than they had initially thought. It seemed to be a combination of advanced technology and ancient magic, a fusion that defied their understanding.

As they delved deeper, they discovered hidden compartments and intricate mechanisms that seemed to defy the laws of physics. Every part was crafted with precision, and they began to appreciate the genius that had gone into its creation. They could only imagine the power that this machine might hold when it was fully operational.

The war had already lasted far longer than imaginable, and in November of 1943, there was no end in sight. After weeks of trying to create a copy based on the original design with little to no success, they decided to take a different approach. After much discussion, they brought in highly skilled engineers and began designing a similar device based on the technology currently available.

This involved finding sound and electronic specialists to duplicate the device's basic principles, frequency modulation combined with vibrational acoustics. They didn't have the time to figure out the rare earth magnets, crystals and tuning forks that worked in harmony to create waves of energy. They brought in existing frequency generators and created a vibrational chamber inside of a metal cylinder, but how the Aetheral harmonic blue rings were formed completely eluded them. This wasn't an easy task. The unit would have to be tethered to a modern power source, not depend on beryl crystals, but shielded from the powerful magnetism of the weapon.

One day, one of the engineers was playing with the broken beryl crystal, and another technician sitting beside him was tuning various frequencies to match the tuning forks. Suddenly, the crystal reacted and started to glow. One engineer yelled out, "Something's happening. Come over here."

The engineer's curiosity and persistence had paid off, and this breakthrough filled the team with a renewed sense of purpose. As John and Richardson approached, they saw the crystal's soft glow, a stark contrast to the dull metal surroundings. The technicians carefully adjusted the frequencies, and the crystal's radiance intensified, emitting a hum that seemed to resonate with the very fabric of the room. They had accidentally stumbled upon a key component of the machine's power source.

As the team worked to understand this phenomenon, they realized that the crystal's reaction was influenced by the specific harmonic frequencies produced by the tuning forks. It seemed that the ancient builders had harnessed a unique form of energy, one that modern science had yet to fully grasp. The team's excitement was palpable as they delved into this new area of exploration, eager to unlock the full potential of their discovery.

With this new lead, the team felt they were on the cusp of a major breakthrough. They began to experiment with different combinations of frequencies and crystals, seeking to replicate the harmonic rings they had seen in ancient texts and etchings found within the machine. The war loomed large, but their dedication to unravelling this ancient mystery remained unwavering.

"I think the key to this is the beryl crystal; we have the tuning forks, and we can construct the copper rings that rotate," the engineer explained.

"Does anyone know where to find beryl crystals?" Richardson asked.

"Yes, I think I know where several may be located," said Jan, "but I don't know how to read the map."

"What map?" Lieutenant Coleman asked.

"This one," with that, Van Rijckenborgh showed them a map from one of the manuscripts.

"Can I take a look?" said Eileen.

"Of course," said Jan, "I want everyone to see this, the more eyes the better." Jan explained that the middle symbol at the top of the map stood for crystal, and on the side were letters.

"That's Gaelic," Richardson said. "I think it means Blue."

As the others looked on, Eileen was concentrating on the Rosicrucian symbols that adorned the edges and the cross-connecting lines that intersected the middle drawing, "That symbol in the drawing. I've seen it before, John. It's the same one on the wall in the village. Remember I pointed it out to you the first night we were there, and when I showed Angus, he said it was an old smuggler's carving."

"Which means," John said with excitement, "we have to go back to Rosslyn and show Angus the map; he may know where it leads and where the beryl crystal might be hidden."

"Well done, Eileen, you would be up for a promotion if you were regular Navy," Arthur Coleman remarked.

"I'll have a car take you two to the train station first thing, and Van Rijckenborgh, you'll need to accompany them."

24

Treasure Hunting

Eileen, John and Van Rijckenborgh set off early the next morning, eager to return to Rosslyn and consult with Angus. The train was on time, and the journey was full of hope. There were candles and Christmas wreaths in the windows of some of the houses in the village, and a picture of Father Christmas on the door of the little school. Eileen thought briefly of Jeffrey, who would have been almost three, and she hoped the gifts she had sent off to her husband would arrive safely.

They made their way to Angus' cottage, hoping he could shed some light on the mysterious map. As they approached, they saw Angus pruning a small dormant apple tree in his garden. He looked up as they drew near, a smile spreading across his weathered face.

"Well, if it isn't my friends from the Navy," he called out, setting down his secateurs. "What brings you back to my neck of the woods?"

Eileen introduced Jan, then wasted no time showing Angus the map. His eyes widened as he studied it, his fingers tracing the intricate symbols and markings. "Aye, this'll be a map, all right," he said, his voice full of wonder. "And I do believe I know where it leads."

Eileen continued, "We recently acquired some old Rosicrucian manuscripts from Jan, who is helping us back at Bletchley with the other artifacts we dug up. The beryl crystal in the Glasgow unit is damaged, so we were hoping the map could lead us to another crystal.

A sense of excitement filled the air as Angus talked about the old smugglers' trade. "I haven't seen this map, said Angus, but I know what these other symbols are. This is leading us straight to the castle, and see these markings? This is the tunnel entrance."

"Tunnel?" Jan said, and others said.

"Yes, we have to enter the hidden tunnels that lead to chambers below Rosslyn Castle; to do that, we need to speak to Miss Leitch, the present caretaker. "We'll set out tomorrow morning. I'll meet you at the inn first thing after breakfast," said Angus. "It's a ten-minute walk to the castle, and we can speak to Miss Leitch. We can hope that she will grant us permission to explore the tunnels and chambers."

The next morning, a thick mist clung to the stone buildings, obscuring the path to the inn. Angus decided to meet them for breakfast. "Good Morning, everyone. Did ye sleep well?"

"Yes, but we are very excited about today's adventure," said John.

"Yes," said Van Rijckenborgh, "I knew the Rosicrucians had been in these parts, but there are very few written records."

"True," said Hamish. "It's all passed down orally from elder to elder."

After breakfast, as they started out. The air hung heavy with the scent of damp earth and wood smoke, a typical morning in this corner of Scotland. Eileen hoped Miss Leitch would agree to their quest to explore the castle's secrets, which depended entirely on her decision. The weight of their expedition settled upon her.

As they approached the castle, they could see that centuries of weather and battle scars had taken their toll. Miss Leitch was outside and seemed eager to meet them. She was dressed in a scarlet wool utility frock and sensible shoes. A warm shawl kept her warm against the December air. "Welcome, everyone. I heard you were coming. It sounds exciting, secret service agents and ancient symbols. I don't get many visitors."

John looked at Eileen, confused. "How did she know?"

"My dear friend Angus came over last night to fill me in," she said, grabbing his hand
tightly. "Come, follow me."

The castle's colossal presence struck them as they neared the gateway, its immense scale utterly breathtaking. Pushing open the heavy front door, the first thing they noticed was the grandeur of the castle's entrance hall. The towering ceilings stretched high above them, adorned with intricate carvings and ornate chandeliers. The walls were lined with tapestries depicting scenes of battles and triumphs. Sunlight streamed in through the glass windows, casting patterns across the marble floor. A maid appeared and took their coats.

As their eyes adjusted to the dimmer interior, they could see the soft glow of candlelight flickering from wall sconces and the grand staircase leading up to the upper levels. The air was thick with the musty scent of centuries-old stone and the faint aroma of burning wood. Despite the opulence, there was an eerie sense of emptiness that seemed to hang in the air, as if the castle was hiding secrets within its walls. They were led into the parlour, the sound of crackling wood coming from a huge fireplace provided warmth to the room.

They began to tell her about their journey and what led them to the castle. She was very understanding but not forthcoming about what lay beneath them in the tunnels.

"The owners don't talk about the tunnels and hidden chambers. I was told not to venture down there, and I didn't even know where the entrance was until recently. As you can see, the castle is always in need of repairs and upgrading. A dear friend of mine came over a few days ago to shore up the kitchen floor. He and I went downstairs, looking at the structure, and we came across a hidden door behind an old shelf unit.

"Did you open it?" said Angus.

"We couldn't; it's frozen in time." Miss Leitch replied.

"Why do you think it's a possible tunnel entrance?" said John.

"Symbols on the door above," she said.

"Symbols?" asked Jan Van Rijckenborgh.

"Yes, they are all over this place, and they are like the chapel's decorations – mysterious and spooky," she said.

"Would we be able to take a look at the symbols?" John interrupted.

"Yes, of course, follow me. It's damp, so I think you should put your coats on. Could you please get the coats, Agnes?"

They walked down a hallway to the basement door by the kitchen.

"Would you like a pair of warm boots, Mrs. Green?" said Agnes, quietly materializing by Eileen's shoulder.

"Yes, please, if you have a pair that will fit."

They descended a stone spiral staircase built to last for centuries. The air grew colder, and their breath formed clouds of condensation in the damp environment. Eileen shivered as she pulled her gloves on and tied her coat tighter around her slim frame. Their footsteps echoed off the stone walls. John led the way with a lantern, its flickering light casting eerie shadows on the ancient walls. The group followed closely behind, their eyes darting around to take in their surroundings.

They reached the bottom of the stairs and found themselves in a large chamber. Miss Leitch directed their attention to a section

186

of the wall where the faint outlines of symbols revealed a hidden door. As they drew closer, they could see intricate patterns and markings that seemed to dance in the flickering light.

"These symbols are similar to those on the map," Angus remarked, his voice filled with excitement. "I believe this is the entrance to the tunnels we seek."

John, the practical one, asked, "Do you have the key to open it, Miss Leitch?"

She nodded, producing a large iron key from her pocket. "I found this years ago, hidden in a chest that I dug up while gardening. I tried every lock in the castle, and it didn't fit any of them, let alone work. She gave the key to John. "Let's see if it works in this door".

He inserted the key and tried to turn it, but the mechanism wouldn't budge. "Do you have any oil, Miss Leitch?" said Angus.

"Yes, I have an old oil can."

"That'll do,"

Angus covered the key with oil and worked it into the lock. After a few tries, it turned, but the door hadn't opened in a long time, so they worked a little oil into the hinges, and eventually, the door creaked open, revealing a long passageway. The basement air was quickly drawn in, which meant there was an opening somewhere further along in the tunnel.

"This is exciting," said Eileen, "Who wants to go first?"

John's response was that of caution. "Before we venture down this path, we need to be better prepared for what may lie ahead."

"I agree said Angus. Let's get some supplies together and return tomorrow, if that's convenient for you, Miss Leitch," John said.

"Yes, of course, she replied, adding, "Oh my goodness, it's time for my morning tea. I baked some fresh scones this morning.

Would you care to join me?" They headed back to the parlour, and Miss Leitch went into the kitchen where Agnes was preparing tea.

Eileen decided to join her. "Have you been living here long?" she asked.

"About ten years now, our family has been connected to the Sinclair Family, who have owned the land for over 900 years. We have been working for the family for four generations, taking care of the grounds and maintaining the castle. When my brother died three years ago, the Sinclairs were kind enough to keep me on. It's been hard to keep everything in working order, but the Earl is very kind and provides the necessary tradespeople to keep things going.

Eileen and Miss Leitch followed Agnes as she carried the tea tray into the parlour, and they all had tea and scones with a little jam before heading back to the inn.

Back in the town, they assembled their supplies. The following morning, they met once more at the castle, ready to embark on their underground exploration. Miss Leitch greeted them warmly, her curiosity piqued by their mysterious endeavour. As they descended into the basement, the air grew colder, and the flickering lantern light cast an eerie glow on the ancient walls. They reached the hidden door, its symbols glowing faintly, beckoning them onward.

With a creak, the oiled door swung open, revealing a long, dark passageway. Eileen, John, Van Rijckenborgh, and Angus stepped through the doorway, their hearts pounding with anticipation. The tunnel stretched before them, its walls lined with ancient stones, the ceiling arching high above. As their eyes adjusted to the dim light, they noticed strange carvings on the walls, the meanings of which were long forgotten.

As they ventured further into the tunnel, the air grew colder, and their breath formed clouds in the lantern light. The musty scent of damp earth and stone surrounded them, and the sound of their footsteps echoed off the ancient walls. Strange symbols and carvings adorned the tunnel, their meanings long forgotten, adding to the air of mystery. The group couldn't help but feel a sense of awe as they realized they were treading a path unseen by human eyes for untold years.

Eileen, indulging her curiosity, ran her gloved hand along the wall, tracing the intricate patterns. "I wonder who carved these and what stories they tell," she mused aloud.

John reminded them to stay focused and alert for any potential dangers that might lurk in a place no one had visited in decades. Their footsteps slowed as they approached a bend in the tunnel, the faint light of the lantern revealing a large, arched doorway. The symbols above the entrance were more intricate and detailed than any they had seen before, and a sense of anticipation hung heavy in the air. With a deep breath and a steady hand, Angus pushed open the heavy iron door. It creaked on ancient hinges, revealing a spacious chamber beyond. The room was filled with a soft, ethereal light emanating from an unseen source. Their eyes widened as they took in the sight before them: a hidden sanctuary untouched by time.

Their lanterns cast shadows on what appeared to be a large stone altar. The light was very dim as they examined the details in the chamber, trying to find a clue to the location of the beryl crystals.

Jan spoke up, "The symbols on the map tell of hidden containers in the altar."

"In this altar?" Angus said, pointing to the stone slab with his torch. Everyone gathered around the stone slab and examined the carvings. John was touching each one to see if they were carved into the slab or if they were separate. There were six eight-inch diameter symbols, and each one was different.

"What do these mean, Van Rijckenborgh?" John questioned.

"From what I can tell, they are all symbols representing power," Van Rijckenborgh replied.

"Power as in the artifact?" Replied John.

"Not sure at this point," Van Rijckenborgh replied. "I think we need to find out where the possible connection is to the hidden container and the power symbols."

John kept fiddling with one of the symbols, and suddenly, it turned clockwise, and a bronze cylinder covered in Rosicrucian symbols sprang up, stirring up quite a bit of dust.

"My goodness gracious," Eileen shouted out.

Jan and the others were astonished.

"Is this what we are after?" asked Eileen.

"I don't know," Van Rijckenborgh responded, "but if this cylinder and the others contain crystals, then it will be a successful mission."

John and Angus discovered that the object was spring-loaded at the bottom, so they proceeded to turn the other five symbols very carefully to release the cylinders. After all the cylinders were out and placed on the altar, they began to search for any other hidden compartments. Jan kept reading the map's notes to determine a way to open the cylinders. He found no immediate solution.

"I think we need to get them out of here and back to the team at Bletchley. Could you get permission from Miss Leitch, Angus? Perhaps she'll also have an old box or crate we could use to hold the cylinders?"

Angus was gone for some time, persuading Miss Leitch that the objects were important to the war effort, that they would keep the cylinders safe, and that John would provide her with a receipt for the material.

John and Angus carefully placed the stone tops back over the holes on the altar, and they made their way back to the castle's basement. After packing the cylinders into an old apple crate, they thanked Miss Leitch for her hospitality and left.

25

The Cylinders'
Secrets are Revealed

They transferred the six cylinders into a secure crate and caught the last train south that evening. Van Rijckenborgh and Eileen read the map's notes and attempted to decipher the codes and symbols for some time before sleeping for a few hours, so they could work when they arrived at Bletchley.

They were picked up at the station by security and driven back to Bletchley, where they placed the crate in Hut 7 and reported to Lieutenant Coleman. Within the hour, Major Williams called a meeting with Eileen, John Van Rijckenborgh, and the two professors to be debriefed about the trip and what they had found. John took the lead as usual and explained the journey into the tunnels, the hidden chamber, and the discovery of the six cylinders with three rings at the top, each engraved with Rosicrucian symbols all around their diameter.

"It sounds potentially dangerous," said Williams.

"We were fine, Major," Eileen said with perhaps more confidence than she had felt at the time.

"Well, where do we go from here?" said the Major.

Van Rijckenborgh said, "Well, Major, I have been studying the map and the notes with Eileen, and I have a strong feeling that the beryl crystals are sealed inside the cylinders, but we haven't discovered a way to open them."

The major suggested using the portable X-ray machine they had obtained to X-ray the larger unit to see what was inside, which might offer a clue. So, John and Professor Richardson were driven out to the abandoned airfield, where they were able to X-ray the unit and develop the glass plate, which revealed several honeycomb-shaped objects and a complicated mechanism that locked the lid.

Van Rijckenborgh and Eileen spent the rest of the day trying to figure out a way to open the cylinders. Realizing that they had been working for a long time without eating, John sent one of the men to a local pub to purchase food.

"Fish and Chips. Get 'em while they're hot." Excited and hungry, they all gathered round the main table and sat down to enjoy the meal. As they were handing out the portions, Eileen grabbed the bottle of vinegar to season her fish and chips. The lid came off, and vinegar spattered across that end of the table and landed on one of the cylinders.

Everyone jumped up to clean it up as quickly as possible. Then Van Rijckenborgh suddenly yelled out, "DON'T MOVE! Look at the top, symbols." A series of three symbols appeared on the lid of the cylinder.

They quickly wrote them down as they started to fade. "That was brilliant, Eileen," said Richardson.

"Well, thank you, Professor."

Richardson, took a fine brush and dipped it in the vinegar, carefully brushing the top of the other cylinders revealing their codes, then Jan got to work, turning the rings to a small notch in the lid to match the symbols on the side of each ring, but the lid was still locked.

Then, Richardson said, "I have a safe back at the university, and you have to turn the wheel several times in one direction and then back in another direction."

"Good thinking, Professor," Van Rijckenborgh remarked. After about an hour, they were successful. Turning the top ring three turns clockwise, the second two counterclockwise, and the third back to line up the other remaining symbols caused the cylinder lid to spring open.

Everyone cheered as the cylinder revealed its secrets. It contained 100 hexagonal-shaped (honeycomb) crystals.

"This is a pivotal moment," said Richardson. "If we can create the magnetic rings and duplicate the running mechanism, we may be able to deploy the technology in hundreds of scenarios."

"Yes," said Eileen, "Six hundred scenarios if my math is correct. I can think of a few right now. If we could adapt the basic principle of the frequencies and harmonics, we would be able to disguise it and maybe integrate it into existing machines, like vehicles and weapons, etc."

"Let's come up with a few ideas that we could implement fairly quickly to present to the Major for possible funding," Mitchell responded.

Then one of the engineers interjected, "With the smaller crystals, we would be able to create a more compact version and control it from an external power source."

"We could even design a directional beam that we could point to, say, an aircraft in flight or a convoy of trucks," said Richardson, "and if we can disrupt signals, one of the best uses would be transmission towers or radar installations."

"Brilliant," said Eileen, "Let's create a formal report for the major and see if we can obtain funding."

Just then, the Major stopped in to see everyone cheering.

"Looks like you have something to celebrate. Would you care to share the news?" Everyone calmed down, and Eileen approached the Major. "Sir, we have managed to crack the code and open the cylinders, revealing what we feel could be a turning point in history. We'll have a report for you in the morning, but John will give you the short version."

John's outline left the Major equally excited. Understanding the significance of this development, the Major promised his full support.

They wasted no time in exploring the full potential of their invention. The ability to disable vehicles and machinery with such precision and ease was a game-changer, and they knew they had to act quickly to stay ahead of the enemy.

And there it was, the goal of all their efforts. A weapon which could end the war!

In due time, the Major made discreet arrangements, the appropriate people were convinced, resources were allocated, and key political figures were notified. The Prime Minister's office was eventually briefed, and the gears of government began to turn slowly.

The group's efforts had opened a world of possibilities.

But the war ended before any of it could be put into production.

During and after the war the OSRD (Office of Scientific Research and Development) and the OSS (Office of Strategic Services) worked on numerous, often unknown projects, many of which remain unrevealed due to the sheer volume of documents and the sensitive political nature of some topics.

The Aether harmonic disruptor has remained to this day a TOP SECRET classified weapon.

After the War

I want to tell you that John Mitchell became a renowned figure in military intelligence, overseeing the expansion of the project and ensuring that the technology was adapted for various applications. When the war ended in 1945, John's efforts were recognized, and he was promoted to a senior position within MI5.

I would also like to tell you that: Angus Hines, the eccentric Scottish historian, continued on with life, always keeping an eye out for suspicious characters; that Finlay, the young Scottish lad, joined the military and served with distinction; that Hamish, the local inn owner, provided a welcoming haven for travellers and soldiers alike; that Callum McGinity, the rustic farmer, tended to his land, proud of his Scottish heritage; that Albert Schultz, the double agent, disappeared without a trace, his loyalties always questionable; that Professor Richardson and Professor Beattie, the astute academics, continued to educate and inspire students at the university; and that Major Williams and Lieutenant Arthur Coleman served with honour, their leadership contributing to the ultimate victory.

Unfortunately, they are all fictional characters.

My mother, Eileen Green, however, is not fictional. She played a crucial role in the war effort. Her analytical skills and quick thinking saved countless lives, and her contributions were not forgotten. She continued to work in naval intelligence at Whitehall and never spoke about her work to anyone.
After the war, Eileen was reunited with her husband, Tom. After six years of trying to adjust to England's post-war devastation and being unable to find a home or steady employment, they decided to emigrate to Canada in 1951.

I did not learn, until she was 94 years old, about her job in Churchill's bunker at Whitehall as a Naval Stores coordinator, supplying the merchant Navy with provisions to the ships in the North Atlantic. I asked her one day for her veteran's number so that I could hire help with cleaning her apartment, and that's when I found out that women who signed up for the Secret Service didn't exist. That's when she told me what her job was during the war.

The Rosicrucian connection and adventures in Scotland are purely fictional, but her job at Whitehall was real.

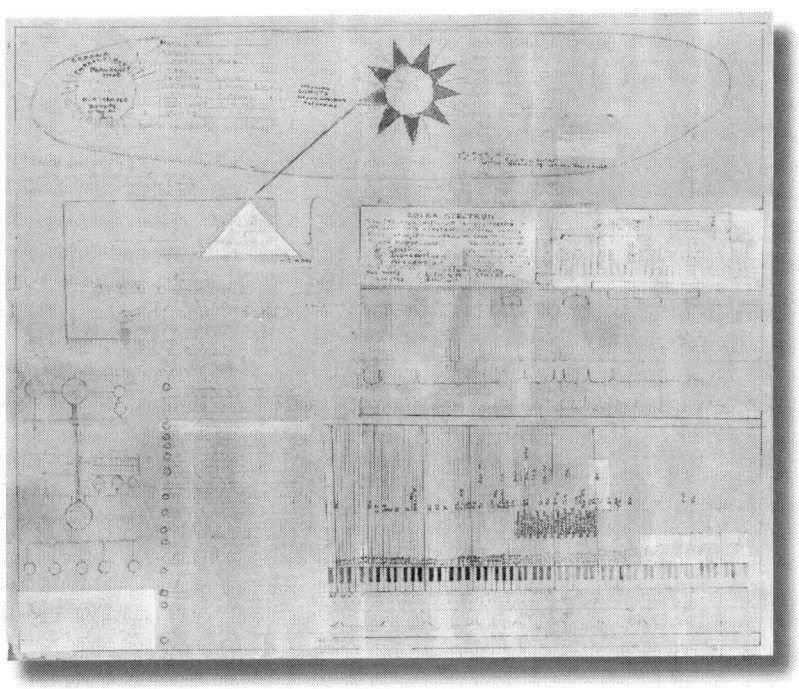

This is the original Rosicrucian diagram that triggered the fictional
journey into the mystic. It belongs to my high school friend Brian
Davis. His grandfather created this over 60 years ago.
His name was Gabriel Davis.

The Rosicrucian
Aether Harmonic Disruptor

Rosslyn Station

Rosslyn Inn

Rosslyn Castle

199

Rosslyn Chapel

Bletchley Park

University of Edinburgh

My mum and I on her 95th birthday in May of 2010.
She passed away in March of 2015, two months
shy of her 100th birthday.

In 2009, I made a 10 minute recording of her story.

Watch on Youtube mumsww2job

https://www.youtube.com/watch?v=ZNY9mMfV1vY

About the Author

Keith Green is heavily involved in his community, having served as a former Firefighter and Rotarian. He has owned several local businesses over the past 51 years. He is presently the President and Board Chair of the Dundas Museum and Archives in Dundas, Ontario, Canada.

Manufactured by Amazon.ca
Bolton, ON